# Party Planning for Introverts

Richard Lowe

The Writing King

**Party Planning for Introverts**

# Table of Contents

See books by Richard Lowe at

https://masterofworlds.com


Get free publishing insights and industry updates at

https://thewritingking.substack.com


For ghostwriting and book coaching services see

https://thewritingking.com

# Dedication

To Erika, Mardhavi, and Jannah, my belly dancer friends who stepped in when grief threatened to silence me forever. After Claudia passed away, when I thought I'd never know happiness again, you helped me remember that bringing people together could be part of healing. Erika, thank you for being the MC when my introvert voice failed me, and for always knowing exactly what needed to happen next.

To Elizabeth of She'endra, whose home became my party university. Thank you for opening your doors so generously and showing me that hosting could be both elaborate and effortless, that gatherings could be both planned and spontaneous.

You all taught me that great hosting isn't about perfect execution; it's about generous hearts, inclusive spirits, and the courage to bring people together around the things that make life more beautiful. When I needed it most, you showed me that community could be a lifeline.

This book exists because you showed me what was possible, even in the darkness.

# Preface

Hi there, fellow introvert.

If you picked up this book, you're probably staring at the same question that haunted me for years: how do you throw amazing parties when the very thought of hosting makes you want to hide under a blanket with a good book? How do you create memorable gatherings when small talk feels like torture and you need three days to recover from a dinner party?

I'm here to tell you that not only is it possible, it might just be your secret superpower.

I'm a raging introvert who has somehow ended up throwing parties in the most unlikely places you can imagine. I've hosted gatherings in a pirate shop surrounded by treasure chests and ship wheels, taken over bars for themed celebrations, convinced municipal spaces to let me throw elaborate dinner parties, and even turned botanical gardens into magical evening venues. I've had events catered by professional services and hired people with food businesses to create intimate dinner experiences that felt both personal and polished.

But here's what nobody tells you about party planning: the most memorable gatherings aren't the ones with the biggest budgets or the most elaborate decorations. They're the ones where people feel welcomed, where conversations develop naturally, and where the host creates space for authentic connection to happen. And introverts? We're naturally brilliant at this stuff.

I've been to Star Trek parties where people debated Federation policy with the same intensity others reserve for actual politics. I've attended Star Wars celebrations that felt like stepping into the cantina scene, complete with costumes that put movie props to shame. I've danced at belly dance parties that transformed living rooms into Middle Eastern fantasies, splashed through mermaid-themed gatherings that made grown adults believe in magic again, and sat transfixed at parties where musicians created impromptu concerts that left everyone in tears.

I've celebrated at religious gatherings that honored tradition while embracing joy, attended Xena parties where warrior princesses ruled the night, and been to events thrown by musicians that felt like private concerts with my closest friends. What made each of these gatherings special wasn't elaborate production values or endless entertainment; it was the thoughtful attention to creating experiences where people could connect around things they genuinely cared about.

The secret I learned through all these experiences is that introvert hosting skills are exactly what most parties are missing. While extroverts focus on high energy and constant entertainment, introverts excel at the things that matter: noticing when someone feels left out, creating comfortable environments where people can be themselves, planning thoughtfully so nothing important gets forgotten, and supporting the kind of meaningful conversations that people remember for years.

Your tendency to plan ahead obsessively? That's not anxiety; that's strategic thinking that prevents problems before they happen. Your preference for smaller, intimate gatherings? That's not antisocial; that's creating space for genuine connection. Your need to understand what makes each guest comfortable? That's not overthinking; that's emotional intelligence that makes people feel truly welcomed.

So settle in with your favorite beverage, find a quiet corner, and let's figure out how to turn you into the kind of host whose parties people want to attend, including you.

# Introduction: Welcome to Introvert Hosting

Let me guess. You're reading this book because someone suggested you host a party, and instead of excitement, you felt that familiar knot in your stomach. Maybe it was your turn to host book club, or your partner gently hinted that it might be nice to have people over, or you realized you've been to seventeen dinner parties this year without reciprocating once. And now you're wondering if there's a way to throw a party that doesn't involve three weeks of anxiety, two days of frantic preparation, and one very long night of pretending to be someone you're not.

I used to think hosting required me to transform into some sparkly, high-energy version of myself. I'd spend parties bouncing around like a caffeinated golden retriever, making sure everyone was having fun while slowly dying inside from social exhaustion. By the time the last guest left, I'd collapse on my couch and need three days of solitude to recover from four hours of "being on."

The turning point came during a disastrous housewarming party where I invited way too many people, tried to cook an elaborate menu I'd never attempted before, and spent the entire evening feeling like I was failing at being a proper host. I was hiding in my bedroom, having a small breakdown about the fact that I'd run out of ice and someone had spilled wine on my carpet, when my friend David knocked on the door.

"This is a great party," he said, finding me stress-eating leftover cheese and crackers. "Everyone's having such a good time."

I stared at him like he'd lost his mind. "Are we at the same party? The one where I forgot to buy enough wine and the playlist stopped working and I haven't talked to half the people here?"

"Yeah, that one," he said. "It feels really relaxed and genuine. People are talking to each other instead of just making small talk. And that thing you did where you introduced Emma and Jake because they both love hiking? They've been talking for an hour."

That's when I realized I'd been measuring my hosting success by extrovert standards. I thought a good party meant I had to be the center of attention, the energetic entertainer, the person making sure every moment was filled with activity and excitement. But what I was good at was creating spaces where people felt comfortable being themselves, where conversations could unfold naturally, and where the shy person in the corner got included without feeling put on the spot.

The best parties I've hosted since then have been the ones where I stopped trying to be an extroverted host and started being an introverted one. Instead of flitting around making sure I talked to everyone, I had a few deeper conversations with people I genuinely wanted to catch up with. Instead of planning elaborate entertainment, I created cozy spaces and let people entertain themselves. Instead of staying "on" all night, I gave myself permission to take breaks, to step outside for a few minutes of quiet, to help with dishes as a way to decompress.

That's what this book is about. Not how to become someone else. How to throw better parties as exactly who you are.

## The Abandonment Loop

Before we get into any of this, I need to name something that doesn't appear in most party planning books because most of them assume you'll actually throw the party.

Here's the pattern. You think: I should have people over. The idea feels good. You start mentally planning: who to invite, what to cook, maybe you pick a date. You feel briefly like a person who hosts parties. Then the voice starts.

It starts small. Are you sure people will want to come? What if nobody responds? What if they come and it's awkward and you run out of things to say and the food is wrong and everyone can tell you don't really know what you're doing?

And you think: maybe not this weekend. Maybe when things are less busy. Maybe when I have a better apartment, a bigger table, more energy, more confidence, more of whatever thing I think I'm currently missing.

The idea dies. You feel a small, specific kind of relief, and a larger, slower kind of disappointment in yourself. And then a few weeks later, you think: I should have people over.

If you've done this loop once, you've done it twenty times. The party that never happened becomes proof that you're not a hosting person. Except you want to be. That's why you're reading this book.

Here's what I've learned about breaking the loop: the voice wins during planning because planning is entirely internal. There's nothing at stake yet. You can abandon the idea with no consequences, no witnesses, no evidence it ever existed.

The intervention is to create a consequence before you're ready. Send one text. Not 'I'm thinking about having people over sometime.' Send an actual message: 'Are you free Saturday the 15th for dinner?' You don't have to know the menu. You don't have to have figured out the logistics. You just have to send it.

Once one person says yes, the party is real. Real things are much harder to abandon than ideas. The voice doesn't disappear, but now it's arguing against something that already exists, which is a much harder case to make.

Everything in this book is about what happens after you send that text. But none of it matters if you never send it. So before you read another chapter, think of one person you've been meaning to have over. You don't have to invite them today. But notice that you're thinking about them.

There's a different version of the abandonment loop that happens later in the process, not before you've committed, but after. The invitations are sent. People are coming. And then somewhere between two weeks out and the day before, the anxiety becomes physical. You can't think clearly about the menu. The guest list that seemed fine now seems wrong. You start looking for a reason to cancel that would sound legitimate.

This is when some people call a friend, not to get advice, not to be talked into anything, but just to say: I'm in the spiral and I need someone to sit with me while it passes. That's it. Not problem-solving. Not reassurance that it'll be great. Just someone who knows you well enough to stay on the phone while you work through the noise in your head out loud.

Here's what that call actually sounds like: you say 'I'm about to cancel and I need you to stay on the phone with me for fifteen minutes.' Your friend will probably ask what's wrong. You will probably have to say something like 'I'm panicking about six people coming over for pasta.' This will feel ridiculous. Say it anyway. The thing about naming it out loud to someone who isn't going to catastrophize with you is that it immediately shrinks. You've been alone with this thought in your head where it has room to grow. Once it's out, it's just a thing you said, and your friend is just a person who heard it, and neither of you died. You don't have to explain further or justify the anxiety or convince them it's real. You just talk, about the party, about something else, about nothing, until the spike passes. It will pass. It always does. Then you hang up and go check on something in the kitchen, because movement helps and the kitchen is where you go when you need a minute. The party starts in four hours. You're going to be fine.

If you have a friend like that, use them for this. Tell them explicitly: I don't need you to fix it, I just need to talk until the anxiety settles. Most people who love you will do this without hesitation. And the anxiety almost always does settle, not because anything changed, but because you moved it from inside your head to somewhere outside it, even briefly.

The party on the other side of that phone call is usually the one you're most glad you threw.

## When You've Already Committed and Still Want to Cancel

Some people don't struggle with the pre-commitment loop. They struggle with what comes after. The invitations went out, people said yes, the date is on the calendar, and now the anxiety is worse than it was before, because now there are real consequences.

If this is you, you've probably cancelled on your own party before. Not with the original group of people. With yourself. You've faked illness. You've invented a work emergency. You've sent the message at 4 PM the day of, hating yourself the entire time you typed it.

Sending the text isn't the intervention for you. You've already done that. Your problem is the gap between commitment and follow-through, and that gap can be days or weeks wide.

A few things that actually help at this stage:

Tell someone you trust what you're planning, and ask them to check in the day before. Not to talk you out of cancelling, just to ask how you're feeling about it. Having one person who knows makes it harder to disappear quietly. The accountability isn't about guilt. It's about having a witness who cares.

Shrink the event in your head if not in reality. The party in your imagination has grown. It's elaborate, high-stakes, and you'll be responsible for every moment of it. The actual party is a few people at your home having dinner. Let the imagined version collapse back down to its actual size.

Make the day-of as easy as possible in advance. If you're going to spiral the morning of your party, do it in a house where everything is already done. Prep as much as you can the day before so that cancelling requires more effort than continuing. The lazier path should be to go through with it.

If you do cancel: don't disappear. Reschedule in the same message. 'I'm so sorry, I'm not able to do Saturday after all. Are you free the following weekend?' This keeps the thing alive instead of killing it. The party you cancelled is still going to happen. It's just happening later.

The goal isn't one successful party. It's breaking the pattern of cancellation that has its own momentum. Each time you follow through, even imperfectly, even with the wrong food and too many awkward silences, you make it harder for the voice to win next time.

# Why Introverts Make Amazing Hosts

Before we get into this, I need you to do something. Take a breath and repeat after me: my introversion is not a problem to be solved. Good. Now let's talk about why it's actually the thing that's going to make you a genuinely excellent host.

Stop me if you've heard this one before: introverts are bad at parties. We're the wallflowers, the ones who hide in bathrooms scrolling through our phones, the people who leave early with mysterious "headaches." We're antisocial hermits who would rather stay home with a book than deal with the exhausting nightmare of small talk and forced social interaction.

Here's the thing about that stereotype: it's complete garbage.

Don't get me wrong, I understand where it comes from. I've been that person at parties, checking my watch every fifteen minutes and calculating how long I need to stay before I can politely escape. I've perfected the art of looking busy by helping with dishes just to avoid another conversation about the weather. I've definitely hidden in a few bathrooms, not because I'm antisocial, but because sometimes you need thirty seconds of quiet to recharge your brain.

But somewhere along the way, we started confusing "needs alone time to recharge" with "terrible at hosting," and that's where we went off the rails. Introverts have superpowers when it comes to throwing parties. We just don't always recognize them as such.

## You Notice Everything

Remember the last party you went to? I'm betting you noticed things that completely flew under the radar for everyone else. You saw that the host's dog was getting overwhelmed by all the attention and needed a break. You noticed that Marcus was standing by himself looking uncomfortable, or that Elena kept glancing at the door like she was planning her escape route. You picked up on the fact that the music was a little too loud for conversation, or that someone had monopolized the snacks table and other people were too polite to squeeze in.

This hyperawareness isn't just an interesting personality quirk. It's a hosting superpower that you can use strategically. But most introverts don't know how to translate their observations into action.

Here's what I do: every few minutes during a party, I run a quick mental sweep of the room. I'm looking for three things: energy mismatches (the overwhelmed person in a high-energy conversation, or the energetic person stuck with quiet talkers), social isolation (someone standing alone or looking uncomfortable), and resource depletion (empty glasses, depleted food, music too loud).

The key is having a response ready for each category. For energy mismatches, I have what I think of as conversation bridges: specific phrases that let me redistribute people without being obvious about it. 'Marcus, you have to hear Elena's story about her trip to Iceland' gets both people engaged in something interesting. 'David, can you help me grab more wine from the kitchen?' rescues someone from a conversation they're clearly done with.

For social isolation, I've learned that direct introductions often backfire because they put people on the spot. Instead, I mention something about the isolated person when talking to someone else nearby: 'Oh, Rachel just got back from that photography workshop you were asking about.' This gives them a natural conversation opener without forcing interaction.

For resource issues, I've developed systems that look like good hosting but are really observation management. I keep backup supplies in strategic locations so I can fix problems quickly. I keep the music volume control easily accessible. I know which conversations are going well and shouldn't be interrupted, and which ones need intervention.

The difference between introvert and extrovert observation is that extroverts notice and react in the moment. Introverts notice, process, and then act strategically. This makes your interventions more effective because they're thoughtful instead of impulsive.

## You Plan Like Your Life Depends on It

Introverts are natural planners. We have to be. While extroverts can wing it and charm their way through social situations, we need structure and preparation to feel comfortable. This might feel like a weakness when you're at someone else's party, but when you're hosting, it's pure gold.

But there's planning, and then there's strategic planning. Most people plan logistics: food, drinks, timing. Introverts can plan psychology.

I spent years arranging furniture wherever it fit and hoping for the best. Then I noticed something: the physical layout of a room almost completely determines what kind of conversations happen in it. That's not abstract; it's directly connected to how much work you end up doing all night.

For example, I never put all the seating in one big circle anymore. That setup forces one group conversation that someone (usually me) has to manage. Instead, I create multiple conversation zones: a 4-person seating area near the fireplace, a standing area around the kitchen island, a quiet corner with two chairs for more intimate conversations. This breaks people into smaller groups that are easier to maintain.

I also seed the space with things worth talking about. A coffee table book about somewhere unexpected. A playlist that's interesting enough to notice but not so weird it becomes the whole conversation. Some small object people haven't seen before. None of it is accidental; I put those things there so conversations have somewhere to land.

I also think in phases. Arrival is higher energy: upbeat music, finger food, people still settling in. Dinner is lower and more focused. Dessert is the natural off-ramp where people can stay in the conversation or start winding down. Planning this in advance means the party has a shape instead of ending badly when everyone's exhausted and no one can figure out how to leave.

Most importantly, I plan my own energy management into the party structure. I know I'll need breaks, so I build legitimate reasons to step away into the timeline. Twenty minutes before dinner, I'll announce that I need to "finish up in the kitchen," which gives me solo task time to recharge. I'll plan a brief toast or group activity that lets me be visible and engaged without having to maintain one-on-one conversations.

## You Create Real Connections

Here's where introverts really shine as hosts: you're not interested in surface-level interactions. You don't want to have the same "How's work?" conversation with fifteen different people. You want to connect with the humans in your space. This preference for depth over breadth transforms the entire atmosphere of your parties.

But creating meaningful connections at parties isn't just about being a good listener or asking thoughtful questions. It requires intentional design and techniques.

My approach is to build in chances for people to share something real before they even arrive. It starts with the invitation. Instead of just "Come for dinner Saturday," I might say "Come for dinner Saturday, I'm making that pasta dish from the place we loved in Rome, and I want to hear about everyone's travel disasters." This primes people to think about stories they want to share.

During the party, I use a threading technique, weaving connections between different people's stories and experiences. When Marcus mentions his photography hobby, I don't just nod and move on. I store that information and later introduce him to David, who also loves photography. But I don't just say "You both like photography." I say "David, Marcus was telling me about this incredible shot he got of the sunrise over the canyon last weekend. Didn't you just get back from a photography trip too?" This gives them content to discuss instead of generic topic overlap.

I've also learned to create a simple progression, starting with low-stakes personal sharing and gradually creating space for more meaningful conversation. This might start with asking people about their favorite local restaurant (safe, personal but not too deep), then moving to travel stories (more personal, good for storytelling), and eventually creating space for people to share things they're excited about or challenges they're working through.

The key is reading the room's comfort level and adjusting accordingly. Some groups will dive deep into meaningful conversation quickly. Others need more time to warm up. Some people will never go deeper than favorite movies, and that's fine too. The goal isn't to force intimacy, but to create opportunities for connection to happen naturally.

I also use interest mapping throughout the party, keeping track of who's interested in what, and creating connections based on genuine shared interests instead of putting people together randomly. This requires active listening and memory work, but it's exactly the kind of social processing that introverts are naturally good at.

## You Know When to Step Back (And When to Step In)

This might be the most underrated hosting skill of all: knowing when you're not needed. Extroverted hosts often feel like they need to be "on" constantly, moving from group to group, keeping energy high, making sure they're visible and engaged with everyone. But sometimes the best thing a host can do is fade into the background and let the party run itself.

But stepping back isn't passive. It's strategic disengagement that requires you to read social cues and make calculated decisions about when your intervention will help versus when it will disrupt natural social flow.

My actual rule is simpler than it sounds: most of the time, do nothing. The hardest skill I've had to build is resisting the urge to jump in when things are fine. Every few minutes I do a quick scan of the room (energy level, who's engaged, who looks stuck) and then I make a call: step in or leave it alone.

The monitoring part comes naturally to most introverts; we're already watching everything. The assessment requires more skill. I look for indicators: Are conversations self-sustaining or dying out? Are people naturally moving between groups or getting stuck? Is the energy level appropriate for the time and activity, or does something need to change?

The action/abstain decision is the crucial part. I act when I see someone struggling (isolated, overwhelmed, or unable to enter conversations), when resources are running low, or when the overall energy needs adjustment. I abstain when conversations are flowing well, when people are successfully managing their own social experience, or when an intervention would be more disruptive than helpful.

For example, if I see two people having an intense conversation in the corner, I don't interrupt just because they've been talking for a while. That's a natural connection happening. But if I see someone hovering near that conversation looking like they want to join but can't find an opening, I might approach and create a bridge: "Are you talking about the hiking trail Elena mentioned? Marcus has done that hike too."

The stepping back part requires confidence in your party design. If you've created good conversation architecture and invited people who are compatible, the party will largely run itself. Your job becomes maintenance and subtle adjustment instead of constant management.

## Your Comfort Zone Is Bigger Than You Think

The biggest lie introverts tell ourselves about hosting is that we're not good at it because it's outside our comfort zone. But here's what I've learned: your comfort zone expands when you're in control of the environment. The anxiety you feel at other people's parties often disappears when you're the one setting the rules.

Willpower alone won't get you there. I know because I tried. I spent a solid year telling myself I'd get better at this by doing more of it. What actually worked was being strategic about what I pushed on.

Start with a simple exercise: identify what makes you uncomfortable about social situations and what makes you feel safe. For most introverts, discomfort comes from unpredictability, forced interaction, inability to recharge, and pressure to be entertaining. Comfort comes from control, preparation, meaningful interaction, and the ability to step back when needed.

Once you know your comfort and discomfort triggers, you can design parties that minimize the discomfort triggers while maximizing the comfort ones. This isn't about avoiding challenges; it's about stacking the deck in your favor so you can take social risks from a position of strength.

I use a gradual expansion strategy, adding one challenging element to each party while keeping everything else within my comfort zone. Maybe I invite one new person to a group of familiar faces. Maybe I try one new activity with a proven guest list. Maybe I extend the party length by 30 minutes with people I trust. This lets me build hosting confidence incrementally instead of jumping into the deep end and burning out.

Hosting confidence is skill-based, not personality-based. You get better at reading rooms, managing group dynamics, and creating connection opportunities through practice and attention, not through becoming more extroverted. Each successful hosting experience expands your comfort zone because you're building evidence that you can handle social challenges effectively.

I also track what works and what doesn't after each party. Not just "did people have fun" but details: Which conversation combinations worked well? What activities generated good interaction? When did I feel most and least comfortable, and why? This data helps me replicate successes and avoid repeating mistakes.

The goal isn't to become comfortable with any social situation, but to become confident in creating social situations that work for you and your guests. That's a much more achievable and realistic target.

Your introversion isn't something to overcome or compensate for when hosting. It's a set of strengths to use strategically. You notice what others miss. You plan for contingencies. You create space for meaningful connection. You know when to lead and when to follow. These aren't consolation prizes for not being naturally outgoing. These are legitimate advantages that make you a host people will remember and want to see again.

# Virtual Parties: A Format Built for Introverts

A note before we get into this: most of what follows applies to any virtual gathering: dinner with friends across time zones, a book club on Zoom, a casual catch-up with people you can't easily get to in person. The last section is specifically for authors hosting book launches, and it's clearly marked. If that's not you, skip it and come back if you ever need it. Everything else is for anyone who has ever thought 'maybe I don't have to do this in person.'

I ran my first virtual book launch party not knowing what to expect. I'd hosted in person plenty of times and assumed virtual would just be a compressed, screen-mediated version of the same thing. What happened instead surprised me. Sixty people showed up. The conversation was sharper than most in-person events I'd hosted. I knew where everyone was the entire time. And when it was over, I wasn't wrecked. I was energized.

Virtual hosting isn't a compromise. For introverts, it's often a more natural fit, and understanding why changes how you approach it.

## Why Virtual Works Particularly Well for Introverts

In-person parties have ambient chaos: people arriving at different times, conversations you can't hear, the constant low-level monitoring of a space you're responsible for. Virtual events compress all of that into a single screen you can see completely at once. You always know who's there. You always know what's happening. For an introvert who runs on observation and preparation, that's not a limitation; it's a relief.

You're also in your own space. Your kitchen. Your chair. Your lighting. The environment you've spent years calibrating for your own comfort. You can have a glass of water nearby, your notes open in another window, the thermostat wherever you want it. The baseline stress that comes from being a guest in your own party, performing in a space that suddenly feels unfamiliar because it's full of people, largely disappears.

The built-in structure helps too. Virtual events have natural time containers: the platform has a start time, people join, people leave. The awkward lingering problem that plagues in-person parties, the guest who won't take any hint that it's time to go, simply doesn't exist. The call ends. Everyone is home already.

And your energy recovery is immediate. When the last person drops off, you're already in your recovery space. No cleanup, no post-party crash in a wrecked apartment. You close your laptop and you're done.

## Platform Choices and Setup

Zoom is the default because everyone has it and nobody needs to be taught how to use it. For most virtual gatherings up to twenty people, it's the right choice. Don't overthink the platform decision; the best platform is the one your guests can join without a tutorial.

A few setup decisions that actually matter:

Lighting. Not a ring light necessarily, but not a window behind you either. A lamp in front of your face, at roughly eye level, makes you look present and engaged. Backlit hosts look like they're in witness protection. It's distracting for everyone.

Sound. A decent headset or earbuds with a microphone will do more for your virtual hosting than any other equipment investment. Built-in laptop microphones pick up every ambient noise in your home and make you sound like you're calling from inside a filing cabinet.

Background. Your actual background is fine if it's not actively chaotic. A blurred background is also fine. An elaborate virtual background that warps every time you move is more distracting than whatever mess is actually behind you.

Camera height. Eye level or slightly above. Camera pointed up at your ceiling is unflattering and creates the impression you're being interrogated. Prop your laptop on books if needed.

For book launches and events with a guest list larger than twenty, consider whether you want a webinar format (host presents, attendees watch and ask questions) versus a meeting format (everyone can speak and be seen). Webinars work better for launches where you want to control the flow. Meetings work better for smaller gatherings where conversation is the point.

## Keeping People Engaged on Screen

The central challenge of virtual hosting is that attention is genuinely harder to hold. People are in their homes, surrounded by their usual distractions, looking at a screen they also use for work and entertainment. The passive guest who would stand politely in a corner at an in-person party will quietly open another tab within ten minutes of a dull virtual event.

The solution isn't to be more energetic or entertaining. It's to give people something to do.

Structured conversation works better than open discussion in virtual settings. Instead of 'does anyone have questions,' try 'I'd love to hear from three people about X, who wants to go first?' Direct invitations work where open invitations create silence. Silence on a video call feels more awkward than silence in a room, and people freeze rather than filling it.

Breakout rooms are underused. For gatherings of more than eight people, breaking into groups of three or four for fifteen minutes creates the kind of conversation that's impossible in a full-group format. People who haven't said a word in the main room suddenly have space to speak. Bring everyone back with a question: 'what was one thing your group talked about?'

Chat is a second conversation happening in parallel. Don't ignore it; acknowledge it. 'I can see in the chat that several people are asking about X' makes people feel heard and gives you material to work with. For book launches especially, the chat fills with reactions and questions that you can surface and respond to in real time.

Shorter is almost always better virtually. Ninety minutes is a long virtual event. Sixty is comfortable. Forty-five is often ideal for launches and presentations. Plan for the time you want, then cut it by fifteen minutes. People will leave appreciating that you respected their attention.

## Managing Your Energy Differently When Hosting Virtually

Virtual hosting is less draining than in-person hosting, but it's not effortless. Screen time has its own fatigue, and the focused attention required to read a room through small video tiles is genuinely tiring in a different way than reading a physical room.

The main difference: you don't need a recharge strategy during the event because the event itself is lower intensity. What you need is a wind-down strategy afterward. The adrenaline of running a virtual event, especially a launch, takes a while to dissipate. Build in thirty minutes of quiet after it ends before you do anything social, even checking messages.

For book launches specifically, the event is often the end of a long preparation period. You've been promoting it, managing RSVPs, preparing content, and fighting your anxiety for weeks. The event itself might be an hour. Plan your recovery for the day, not just the hour.

A few things that matter more for virtual events than most people plan for:

Take the afternoon off before it. Don't schedule a virtual event at the end of a workday. The cognitive load of being on camera, managing your own face, listening, responding, tracking chat, performing presence, is substantial. You need to arrive with something in reserve, not already depleted.

Eat a real meal beforehand. Coffee is not a meal. Your brain is doing a lot of work and it will notice at the 90-minute mark if you didn't give it anything.

If you freeze mid-answer, and someone reading this will, the script is: pause, say 'let me think about that for a second,' take a breath, answer a simpler version of the question. You do not have to perform fluency. A genuine pause reads as thoughtfulness. What tanks a virtual event is a host visibly panicking, not a host visibly thinking.

Build in a 10-minute buffer after the event ends before you do anything else. Don't jump straight to checking messages or decompressing socially. Sit somewhere quiet. The adrenaline will take a few minutes to settle and your assessment of how it went will be much more accurate after it does.

One practical note: have water nearby and drink it. Virtual hosting involves more talking than in-person hosting because you're filling silence that would otherwise fill itself. Your voice will thank you.

## Virtual Parties as a Distinct Format

Virtual gatherings aren't a substitute for in-person hosting; they're a different format with different strengths. Where in-person parties give you physical presence, ambient energy, and the texture of a shared space, virtual gatherings give you something else: everyone visible at once, no ambient chaos to monitor, immediate recovery when it ends. For introverts, those aren't consolation prizes. They're genuine advantages that change what the evening can be.

Book launches, author events, subject-matter discussions, informal catch-ups with friends scattered across time zones: these have their own natural home in the virtual format. Not because in-person wouldn't work, but because virtual often works better on its own terms: attendance is easier, energy is more contained, and the conversation tends to stay on track.

The key is designing them as virtual events from the start, not as in-person events that happen to be on a screen.

Everything in the rest of this book applies to virtual parties. The guest list strategy, the energy management, the conversation bridges, the scripts: all of it translates. The main difference is the medium, not the underlying work of creating a space where people feel welcome and conversations can happen. That part is the same.

## Case Study: The Virtual Book Launch

When I advise authors on virtual book launches, I give them a specific formula that addresses the two biggest problems with author events: time zones and author nerves.

Run it for three hours. This feels long, but it's the only way to serve a US audience across all time zones without asking anyone to join at an unreasonable hour. The key is that the event doesn't require three hours of sustained attention from anyone; guests come and go, and the structure keeps things interesting throughout.

Invite three to five influencers in your book's subject area to appear at staggered intervals, roughly once an hour, for five to ten minutes each. They don't need to prepare much: a brief comment on why the book matters to them, maybe one question for the author, then they're done. Their audiences will tune in for their slot, which means your attendance builds in waves rather than peaking at the start and slowly emptying out. Each influencer appearance is a fresh reason to show up.

Get someone else to act as host. This is the single most important thing an introverted author can do for their own launch, and if you don't have a friend or colleague who can do it, pay someone. A skilled virtual host for a three-hour event typically costs less than your book cover design and is worth every dollar. The host manages the platform, watches the chat, introduces guests, handles the games, and keeps the energy up between segments. The author's job is to be present, answer questions, and talk about the book, not to simultaneously run the logistics of a three-hour live event. Those are two different jobs and they pull in opposite directions. A paid host is not an extravagance. It's the difference between an event you survive and one you actually enjoy.

Run simple games with prizes throughout; signed copies of the book work perfectly. Trivia about the book's topic, a caption contest, a question that requires people to have read the description. Games do three things: they reward engaged attendees, they give the host something to do between segments, and they create a reason for people to stay past the slot they originally planned to attend. Someone who joined for an influencer at the top of the hour will often stay another thirty minutes hoping to win a signed copy.

Here's how the structure works, slot by slot:

Opening twenty minutes: The host welcomes people, explains the format, and handles logistics (chat questions, prize announcements, how breakout rooms will work if you're using them). The author speaks briefly, five minutes maximum, about what the book is and who it's for. Keep it conversational, not a reading. People are still arriving. This is not the moment for your best material.

Q&A sessions: Prepare ten questions in advance and give them to your host. Real audience questions are unpredictable and can die on arrival; prepared questions guarantee the conversation stays substantive. The host asks; the author answers; the host redirects to chat questions when they appear. The author should never be managing the chat while also trying to think and speak.

Influencer slots: Brief the influencer in advance with three specific things: one sentence about their connection to the book's topic, one question they're going to ask the author, and how long they have. Five to eight minutes is plenty. Longer and it becomes a second event inside your event. Their job is to validate the book's value to their audience, hand off to the author for one exchange, and exit cleanly.

Games: Keep them simple enough to run in two minutes. 'First person to type the correct answer wins a signed copy' works. Trivia questions pulled from the book's content work. Caption contests with a book-related image work. The host runs all of this; the author participates as a player, not a facilitator.

The reading or story: Pick one passage or one story from the book's writing process, something that doesn't make sense without context, something that will make people want to read the surrounding pages. Seven minutes maximum. End on a sentence that makes people want to know what comes next.

This formula works because it's designed around how introverted authors actually function under pressure, not how extroverted event hosts do. You don't need to be 'on' for three hours. You need to be genuine for a few concentrated stretches, surrounded by a structure that handles everything else.

The author participates throughout but is never solely responsible for filling the time. There's always a next thing coming. That structure, knowing exactly what happens when, with other people carrying parts of it, is what makes a three-hour event manageable for someone who would otherwise spend the whole time convinced they're about to run out of things to say.

## After the Event: What Actually Moves Books

The event itself doesn't sell books. What sells books is what happens in the 48 hours after. Send a follow-up email the next morning to everyone who registered (not just who attended) with a link to buy, a link to leave a review, and one specific reason why a review matters. Make the review ask personal: 'Reviews from readers like you are what help other introverts find this book when they're searching for exactly what they need.'

Ask your influencer guests to post something, anything, the day after. A quote from the event, a screenshot from the chat, their own recommendation. This extends the event's reach to audiences who weren't there.

Follow up with anyone who asked a substantive question in the chat. A personal message, not a mass email, that references their specific question and offers a short answer or a related passage from the book. This turns attendees into advocates.

Here's what that follow-up email actually sounds like:

**Subject: Thank you for coming, and a small ask**

'It meant a lot to have you at *Event Name* yesterday. If you enjoyed it, the single most useful thing you can do is leave a review, even two sentences, on Amazon or Goodreads. Reviews are how other readers find the book when they're searching for exactly this kind of help. Here's the link: *link*. And if you haven't picked up a copy yet, here's where to find it: *link*. Thank you again.'

Keep it short. Keep the ask specific. One link to review, one link to buy, one sentence explaining why the review matters. People who attended your launch already like you; they just need to be asked directly and given the exact steps. Most won't do it without a prompt, and most will do it with one.

# Designing Parties That Don't Drain You

Quick show of hands: how many of you have hosted a party, smiled through the whole thing, said your goodbyes, closed the door behind the last guest, and then leaned against it like you'd just survived something? All of you. I know. This chapter is about making that collapse optional.

Let's talk about the thing nobody warns you about when you decide to start hosting: the post-party crash. You know the one. It's Tuesday morning, three days after your dinner party ended, and you're still recovering from the social hangover. You're lying in bed wondering why you thought it was a good idea to invite eight people over when you can barely handle a phone call some days.

Here's the plot twist: it doesn't have to be this way.

The reason most introverts feel completely wiped out after hosting is that we're trying to throw extrovert parties with introvert energy systems. We're planning events that require us to be "on" for hours, to engage with everyone constantly, and to maintain high energy levels until the last person leaves. Then we wonder why we need a week of hibernation to recover.

But what if you could throw parties that energize you? Not in some fake "fake it till you make it" way, but in a real "I'm genuinely enjoying this and don't want it to end" way. The secret is designing gatherings around your natural rhythms and energy patterns instead of fighting against them.

## Know Your Social Battery Level

First things first: you need to get honest about your social battery. And I mean really honest, not "I should be able to handle this" honest or "normal people can do this" honest. I mean "what does my energy look like" honest.

Your social battery is not the same as your extroverted friend's social battery. It doesn't charge the same way, it doesn't drain the same way, and it definitely doesn't have the same capacity. Trying to host a party with someone else's energy expectations is like trying to run a marathon when you're trained for a 5K. You might finish, but you're going to feel like garbage.

Here's what actually helped: for two weeks, I tracked my social interactions and energy levels. Before and after each situation (one-on-one coffee, group dinner, work meeting, phone call), I noted how I felt and how long it took to feel normal again.

Here's what I discovered about my own patterns: One-on-one conversations with close friends for up to two hours are energizing (energy goes up). Group conversations with 3-4 people I know well for 2-3 hours are neutral (energy stays stable). Mixed groups of 5-8 people where I know half of them drain me steadily but manageably for about 3 hours before I hit a wall. Groups larger than 8 people or situations where I know fewer than half the people drain me fast; I'm done in 90 minutes max.

I also learned that certain types of people affect my energy differently. High-maintenance friends who need a lot of emotional support drain me faster than low-key people who are fun to be around. Naturally social people who keep conversation flowing preserve my energy. People who dominate conversations or create drama accelerate the drain.

What I do with this information is simple: I stop planning the party I think I should be able to host and start planning the one I can actually host well. Battery lasts three hours? Two-and-a-half-hour party. Need breaks? I build them in as real events, not escapes. Can only hold six real conversations in a night? Six people on the guest list.

This isn't settling or being antisocial; it's strategic energy management. When you plan within your capacity, you can be fully present and engaged for the duration of the event. Your guests get the best version of you instead of the increasingly exhausted one.

The voice that says this is too much analysis for a dinner party is the same voice that makes you fake-smile through five hours of exhaustion while internally counting ceiling tiles. Track your battery once; stop wondering why you're always depleted.

## Build in Natural Transition Points

One of the biggest energy drains for introverts is the feeling that a social situation is open-ended and could go on forever. When you don't know how long something will last, it's impossible to pace yourself. You end up either burning through all your energy early or holding back so much that you're not really present.

What I've learned to do is give the party a shape. Not a rigid schedule: a beginning, a middle, and an off-ramp that everyone can see coming. When there's a natural structure, nobody has to guess when it's okay to leave, and you don't have to manage the ending.

For dinner parties, I've developed a three-act structure with specific timing. Act One is arrival and appetizers (45 minutes max). This gives people time to settle in and start conversations, but prevents the dreaded "standing around awkwardly for two hours while the host finishes cooking" scenario. Act Two is dinner (60-90 minutes depending on the group size and conversation flow). Act Three is dessert and coffee (30-45 minutes), which signals that the evening is winding down and gives people an easy exit point.

The genius of this structure is that it works for different energy levels and social needs. People who want to leave after dessert can do so gracefully. People who want to stay and continue the conversation can migrate to the living room for Act Four: The Sequel. But nobody feels trapped or uncertain about timing.

I use similar structures for other types of gatherings, but with different timing based on the energy requirements. For casual afternoon gatherings: arrival and snacks (30 minutes), group activity (45-60 minutes), open socializing (60 minutes). For holiday parties: arrival and mingling (30 minutes), group tradition or toast (15 minutes), food and conversation (90 minutes), gradual departure window (open-ended but with clear signals).

Each phase should have a different energy requirement. Arrival should be low-pressure. The middle phase can be higher energy. The end phase should naturally wind down. This prevents the common party problem where energy peaks early and then everyone stands around wondering when it's okay to leave.

Here's the practical part: communicate these phases to your guests, but subtly. Instead of announcing "Now we're moving to Act Two," use environmental cues. Dim the lights slightly when transitioning from cocktails to dinner. Change the music tempo. Move people to different spaces. These signals help people adjust their energy accordingly.

## Create Recharge Opportunities

Here's something most hosting advice doesn't tell you: it's okay to take breaks during your own party. In fact, it's not just okay, it's essential. You wouldn't expect your phone to work all day without charging. Why would you expect your social battery to be any different?

The fake break is hiding in the bathroom while mentally running through your hosting checklist. I know because I did it constantly. Two minutes of anxious standing near a toilet isn't rest. A real break looks like: door closed, task in hand, brain off social mode. Even five minutes of that makes a difference.

Real recharge breaks have specific characteristics: they involve solitude or very minimal social interaction, they engage a different part of your brain than party hosting, and they last long enough for your nervous system to reset (usually 5-10 minutes minimum).

The trick is building legitimate recharge opportunities into the party structure so they feel natural. Kitchen time is perfect for this, but only if you do it right. Don't just stand in the kitchen stress-prepping while people wander in and try to help or chat. Instead, announce that you need "10 minutes to get the next course ready" and ask someone else to handle host duties while you're gone. Then spend those 10 minutes doing something restorative: listen to a calming song on headphones, step outside for fresh air, or just stand quietly and breathe.

I also design activities that naturally split the group's attention so I can float between active hosting and passive observation. Photo albums that people can look through while talking. A puzzle that some people can work on while others continue conversation. A playlist that people can add to throughout the evening. These activities reduce the pressure on you to be the constant entertainment source.

Outside space is gold for recharge breaks if you have it. "Checking on the garden" or "getting some fresh air" are socially acceptable reasons to step away. If you don't have outdoor space, create designated quiet zones inside. A reading nook with interesting books. A workspace where you can legitimately "check on something" for a few minutes. The key is having a plausible reason to be alone that doesn't make guests feel abandoned.

Here's the advanced technique: recruit a co-host who understands your energy needs and can provide cover when you need breaks. More on this in the next section, but having someone who can smoothly take over host duties for 5-10 minutes is a game-changer.

Don't feel guilty about needing these moments. You're not being antisocial or rude. You're taking care of yourself so you can be a better host for the remainder of the party. Your guests will have a better time if you're present and engaged than if you're physically there but mentally checked out because you're overwhelmed.

## Recruit Extroverted Co-Conspirators (The Right Way)

Here's the introvert hosting secret that nobody talks about: you don't have to do this alone. In fact, you shouldn't. While you're busy overthinking the menu and worrying about conversation flow, your extroverted friends are probably dying to help you throw an amazing party. They love this stuff. Let them.

But recruiting help requires strategy. You can't just ask someone to "help out" because different people interpret that differently. Some will take over your entire party (not helpful). Others will just stand around waiting for instructions (also not helpful). You need to be specific about what kind of help you want and match tasks to personalities.

The people who help best are the ones who enjoy what you're asking them to do. Three roles consistently work well.

The first is someone who naturally draws people into conversation and helps shy guests feel included. Ask them to arrive 15 minutes early to help with arrivals and introductions. Their job is to make sure no one stands alone and that conversations get started. When you need a recharge break, they take over the social hosting duties.

The second type loves practical work: refilling drinks, managing coats, keeping food stocked, handling music. They get satisfaction from keeping things running smoothly. Give them specific tasks and locations. They enjoy the behind-the-scenes work that you find draining.

The third type is good at reading room dynamics and can tell you when to transition activities, when someone needs rescuing from a conversation, or when the party energy is flagging. They become your co-observer, which doubles your ability to monitor and respond to social dynamics.

Here's how to recruit them: "I'm throwing a dinner party for eight people on Saturday and I could use a co-host. Would you be interested in coming early to help with setup and then being my social wingman during the party? I'm thinking you could help with introductions and keeping conversations flowing while I handle food and logistics."

Most extroverts love this because it gives them a legitimate way to be helpful and social. They're not just attending your party, they're contributing to its success. This appeals to their natural desire to be involved and useful.

The key is being clear about boundaries and expectations. You're not asking them to throw the party for you, you're asking them to complement your hosting style. They handle the high-energy social facilitation; you handle the thoughtful planning and detailed execution. It's a partnership that plays to both of your strengths.

## Choose Your Guest Mix Carefully

Not all social combinations are created equal when it comes to energy drain. Some people are energizing to be around, others are neutral, and some people drain your battery just by existing in your space. When you're planning a party, think strategically about the mix of personalities you're inviting.

But this goes deeper than just "invite people you like." You need to consider how different personalities interact with each other and how much hosting energy each person requires from you.

Before finalizing any guest list, I think about each person in three ways: how much do they help or hinder group dynamics, how much personal attention do they require from me, and how well do they mix with my other friends.

Some guests actively make the party better; they draw quiet people into conversation, ask good questions, create positive energy. These people reduce your hosting workload because they contribute to the social success of the party.

Others are neutral, pleasant, appropriate, fine in any mix, don't require special attention.

And some guests increase your workload significantly; they dominate conversations, create drama, need constant attention, or make others uncomfortable. Not bad people, but high-cost guests.

Hosting energy is separate from group dynamics. Some guests are fine in the room but personally draining to you, the friend going through a divorce who'll want to pull you aside for support, the colleague who's naturally entertaining but high-maintenance. Both require something from you specifically, not just from the room.

Compatibility is about how well people mix with your existing friend groups. Some friends are amazing individually but terrible together. Others bring out the best in each other.

In practice: include at least one person who reliably contributes to group energy, limit high-cost guests to one per party (and only when you're feeling strong), and avoid known compatibility problems. If you're inviting someone who needs a lot of personal attention from you, make sure the rest of the list is low-maintenance.

This isn't about excluding people or being judgmental. It's about understanding that different people require different amounts of your hosting energy, and planning accordingly. Save the high-maintenance guests for times when you're feeling social and energetic. When you're running on a low battery, prioritize people who contribute positive energy to the group dynamic.

## Design Activities That Work for Mixed Personalities (Beyond Small Talk)

The worst kind of party activity for an introvert host is anything that puts you at the center of attention or requires you to maintain high energy for extended periods. Charades, karaoke, and elaborate party games might be fun for some people, but they can be exhausting when you're the one responsible for keeping them going.

But just having "good conversation" isn't enough either. Without some structure, you end up with awkward silences, cliquey subgroups, or the dreaded scenario where everyone is politely waiting for someone else to start talking.

The solution is to build conversation into the environment itself: activities and setups that generate meaningful interaction without requiring you to be the constant facilitator.

Collaborative creation activities work brilliantly for this. Set up a build-your-own taco bar where people work together to create their food. The collaboration breaks the ice naturally and gives people something to do with their hands while talking. Or try a group playlist where everyone adds songs throughout the evening; it creates ongoing interaction and reveals personality through music choices.

Memory sharing activities tap into people's natural love of storytelling. Create a simple photo album from a shared experience (if you're hosting people who know each other from somewhere specific) or set up conversation prompts that invite storytelling: "What's the most interesting place you've been this year?" or "What's something you learned recently that surprised you?"

Optional engagement activities let people participate at their own comfort level. Set up a puzzle that some people can work on while others just talk. Put out interesting books or magazines. Create a question jar where people can pull out conversation starters if they want to. People can engage or not engage based on their own energy and interest.

Skill sharing activities work well when you know your guests' interests. Ask someone who loves photography to bring their camera and take candid shots. Have your friend who's great at cocktails teach everyone to make a signature drink. Let your friend who knows wine lead a casual tasting. This takes pressure off you to entertain while giving guests a chance to share something they're passionate about.

These activities should enhance conversation, not replace it. They provide structure and natural talking points, but the real connection happens in the conversations that develop around the activities.

## Set Realistic Time Boundaries

This is the big one, the boundary that will save your sanity and your social battery: decide how long your party will last and communicate that timeline clearly. Not just to yourself, but to your guests.

I know this feels awkward at first. We're taught that good hosts keep the party going as long as people want to stay, that ending a party early means you're not fun or social enough. But here's the truth: your guests will have a better time at a three-hour party where you're engaged and present than at a six-hour party where you're increasingly exhausted and checked out.

But setting boundaries isn't enough; you need systems to maintain them without feeling guilty or rude.

When I send invitations now, I include specific times and context. "Come for dinner from 6 to 9 PM, we'll eat around 7" or "Join us for Sunday brunch from 11 AM to 2 PM." This sets expectations for everyone, including me. It gives introverted guests permission to plan their energy accordingly, and it gives extroverted guests a clear framework so they don't feel like they're imposing by staying late or leaving early.

Here's the advanced technique: build the ending into the party structure, not just the invitation. About 30 minutes before your planned end time, start winding things down. Serve coffee or tea instead of more wine. Switch to quieter background music. Start a group activity that has a natural ending point, like looking through photos from the evening or doing a group toast.

These environmental cues signal to guests that the party is winding down without you having to make awkward announcements. Most people will start thinking about leaving naturally. For the people who don't pick up on social cues, you have clear permission to say, "I've had such a wonderful time, but I'm starting to wind down for the evening."

The magic happens when you plan parties that end before you want them to. When you're designing a three-hour event but you still have energy left at the end, you feel successful and satisfied instead of depleted and overwhelmed. Your guests leave wanting more instead of staying until everyone is tired and cranky.

If people are having such a good time that they want to extend the gathering, you can always make an exception. But having a planned end time gives you the option to stick to your boundaries if you need to. It's much easier to say "I had such a great time, but I need to start winding down" when you've already communicated the timeline than it is to suddenly announce that people need to leave.

Your energy is not unlimited, and that's not a character flaw that needs to be fixed. It's information that needs to be incorporated into your party planning. When you design gatherings around your capacity instead of your theoretical capacity, you create space for genuine connection and enjoyment. And isn't that the whole point?

# The Guest List Strategy

The guest list is where most parties are won or lost, usually before anyone has eaten a single chip. It's also where introverts tend to make the most well-intentioned, people-pleasing, anxiety-generating mistakes, inviting the person we feel guilty about, the couple where one of them derails every conversation, or simply everyone we know and then quietly dreading each RSVP that comes in. Let's fix that.

Let me tell you about the worst guest list mistake I ever made. It was my birthday party, and I decided to invite everyone I liked. Sounds reasonable, right? College friends, work colleagues, family, neighbors, that person I met at a coffee shop who seemed cool. Thirty-two people total, because why not celebrate big?

What I ended up with was seven different social groups who had absolutely nothing in common, standing around making polite conversation while I frantically ran between clusters trying to facilitate introductions and prevent awkward silences. By the end of the night, I was so exhausted from social traffic directing that I hid in my bedroom while my own birthday party continued without me.

### Start Small and Build Your Hosting Confidence

Here's the truth that no one wants to admit: most people are terrible at estimating how many guests they can handle well. We think in terms of space (my living room fits twelve people) or obligation (I should invite everyone who invited me to their thing) instead of thinking about our actual capacity to create a good experience for each person attending.

Before you add another person to your guest list, ask yourself: can I have a meaningful interaction with each person at this party? Not a quick 'thanks for coming' exchange: an actual conversation where I'm present and engaged. If the answer is no, your guest list is too big.

For most introvert hosts, this number is smaller than you think. I can handle six to eight people comfortably, which means I can have real conversations with everyone, notice if someone needs attention, and still enjoy myself. Ten people pushes my limit. Twelve people means someone is definitely getting ignored, and I'll spend the whole party feeling guilty about it.

But here's the counterintuitive part: smaller parties often feel more intimate and special to guests. When someone leaves your six-person dinner party saying "that was the most fun I've had in months," you've created something memorable. When someone leaves your twenty-person party saying "it was nice," you've created background noise in their social calendar.

Start with four people for your first few parties. Yes, four feels small. Yes, you'll worry that it's not "enough" of a party. But four people plus you creates a perfect conversation dynamic where everyone can be included easily, you can manage the flow without stress, and if one person has to leave early, you still have a viable group.

The voice that says four people isn't a real party is applying extrovert metrics to an introvert skill set. Four people who leave at midnight because nobody wanted to go home is a better party than twenty people who leave at nine because the energy ran out. Ignore it.

Once you've successfully hosted several four-person gatherings and feel confident about the dynamics, add one more person. Then another. But resist the temptation to jump from six people to twelve people just because you're feeling confident. Each additional person doesn't just add one more conversation; it adds exponential complexity to group dynamics.

I track my hosting capacity like athletes track their training progress. After each party, I note how many people attended, how I felt during and after the party, what worked well, and what felt challenging. This data helps me understand my actual limits instead of relying on what I think I should be able to handle.

A note for those who don't have the luxury of starting small: if the party is already planned, the guest list is already large, or the social obligation isn't negotiable, don't close the book. Every concept in this chapter scales. The room-scanning technique works in a room of twenty. The conversation web approach works with twelve people. The energy management strategies matter even more when the stakes feel higher. Start small when you can. When you can't, use the tools anyway.

## When You're Building the Circle, Not Hosting It

Most of this chapter assumes you have people. Friends from work, neighbors you've talked to, a social circle that already exists and just hasn't been to your home. If that's you, skip ahead.

But some people are reading this from a different position. You've moved to a new city. You've come out of a long relationship or a period of isolation. You're starting over in some way. You don't have four people waiting for an invitation; you're still trying to find them. And you're hoping hosting might help.

It can. But it works differently when you're building from scratch.

The first thing to let go of is the idea that a party should celebrate existing closeness. That's one kind of gathering. The kind you're hosting is different; it's an experiment in whether closeness is possible. You're not bringing friends together. You're putting potential friends in a room and seeing what happens.

This means your guest list looks different. It's the woman from yoga you've had exactly one good conversation with. The work colleague who mentioned they also moved here recently. The neighbor whose name you learned two weeks ago. These aren't people you know; they're people you're trying to know. That's the point.

Lower the stakes in every direction. Smaller number, simpler food, shorter evening, lower formality. The goal of this gathering is not a successful party. The goal is one good conversation with one person that makes both of you want to do it again. If you get that, the party worked, regardless of what else happened.

Don't try to host strangers who don't know each other. That's hard even with an established friend group running it. For your first few gatherings from zero, invite people who already have something in common, from the same yoga class, the same company, the same neighborhood. Give them a shared context to fall back on so the conversation doesn't have to start from nothing.

Expect the first one to be imperfect and mostly survive. You're not trying to throw a great party. You're trying to get through one, learn something from it, and have a specific reason to follow up afterward. 'It was so good to finally get you over, we should do it again sometime' is the entire victory condition for gathering number one.

The people who end up at your table six months from now, the ones you can't imagine not knowing, almost none of them will have arrived as close friends. They started as exactly the kind of tentative acquaintances you're inviting. Hosting is how you close that distance. It's just slower than it looks from the outside.

## Mixing Personalities Strategically

The worst parties I've thrown had perfectly good people in them. The problem was the combination. Two people who are both great separately can kill a room together. Two people who'd never meet otherwise can become the center of gravity for an entire evening. Guest list is chemistry, and you're the one running the experiment.

Think about connections, not individuals. Each person needs at least two potential conversation partners: people with shared interests, complementary curiosities, or compatible energy. Start with your most socially comfortable guest, then build outward. Your anchor is Sarah, who loves hiking and works in marketing. Add Marcus, who also hikes. Add Elena, who also works in marketing. Then find someone who connects to Marcus or Elena in a different direction.

Not all connections have to be obvious hobby matches. Shared experiences (same college), similar life stages (both just moved to the city), complementary interests (the photographer and the traveler): these often generate better conversations than two people who do the exact same thing.

Consider not just who people are, but who they become around different people. Your friend who's quiet at work events might be the funniest person in the room with your college group. Think about which version of each person you're inviting, and build the list to bring that version out.

One hard rule: don't invite people who are currently in conflict with each other. You will convince yourself they can be mature for one evening. They cannot.

## RSVP Management Without the Phone Anxiety

Most introverts hate the RSVP follow-up process. The checking-in texts. The anxiety about the maybes. The guilt about chasing people who are probably just being politely noncommittal. Here's how to remove almost all of that: set a deadline on your invitation, make silence count as a no, and stop waiting. Include clear language: "Please reply by *specific date* so I can plan food accordingly; if I don't hear from you, I'll assume you can't make it." It's not rude. It's the only thing that lets you plan.

*Make responding as easy as possible. Instead of asking people to email you back, include specific options: "Reply with YES, NO, or MAYBE." People respond to one word. They do not respond to open-ended requests that require them to think.*

Invite more people than you want. If you want six, invite eight. Last-minute cancellations are inevitable and have nothing to do with you. Also keep a short backup list, people you'd have invited anyway, so if a spot opens up you're not scrambling.

Two days before: "Looking forward to seeing everyone who can make it on Saturday; if your plans have changed, no worries, just let me know." This reduces the guilt that makes people avoid responding. You're giving them an easy out, which paradoxically makes them more likely to actually show up.

For people who consistently don't respond: stop inviting them. Not as punishment, just as math. Your hosting energy is finite.

## Handling Plus-Ones and Last-Minute Changes

The plus-one question is where many introvert hosts get derailed. Someone asks if they can bring their partner, or their visiting cousin, or their new friend you've never met. Your people-pleasing instincts say yes, but your hosting anxiety knows that unknown guests add complexity and unpredictability to your carefully planned gathering.

Here's my framework for plus-one decisions: Consider the impact on group dynamics, your hosting capacity, and the specific person being added. If your party is designed for intimate conversation among people who know each other, adding a stranger changes the entire dynamic. If you're already at your comfort limit for number of guests, adding one more person might push you over the edge.

But the specific person matters too. If your friend wants to bring their long-term partner who's naturally social and gets along well with your friend group, that's different from someone wanting to bring a first date or a friend who's going through a difficult time and needs extra attention.

I've learned to give conditional yeses: "I'd love to meet *partner's name*, but this is going to be a small group of people who all know each other, so it might not be the best introduction setting. Would you rather come solo this time, or should we plan to get together separately so I can meet them properly?" This gives your friend a choice and shows that you're interested in meeting their person, just not necessarily at this specific gathering.

For last-minute additions, I have a simple rule: if adding someone would require me to change my menu, seating arrangement, or party structure, the answer is no. If someone can be smoothly added without disrupting my planning, I consider it. But I never say yes out of guilt or social pressure.

Last-minute cancellations are easier to handle than additions. Build emotional resilience into your expectations by assuming that 10-20% of your guests might cancel day-of due to illness, work emergencies, or life chaos. This is normal and not a reflection on your party or your friendship.

When someone cancels last-minute, resist the urge to find a replacement guest immediately. Your party was planned for the original number of people, and smaller groups often lead to better conversations anyway. Use the extra food as leftovers, or invite your remaining guests to take home care packages.

Flexibility doesn't mean saying yes to everything. True flexibility means having systems that can accommodate reasonable changes without completely derailing your hosting plan.

## Creating Guest Combinations That Spark Natural Conversations

Seeding conversations before people arrive is one of the more useful things I do. When I invite people, I mention something interesting about whoever else is coming. Not in a forced way, just enough that they arrive with a question ready.

I do a version of interest mapping when building guest lists. For each potential guest, I mentally map their interests, experiences, and conversation topics. Then I look for intersections, not the obvious ones, but the less predictable connections that lead to more interesting conversations.

Everyone expects the two people who work in tech to have something to talk about. But what about the person who loves cooking and the person who just got back from a food tour of Italy? Or the person who's training for a marathon and the person who just started physical therapy for a running injury? These connections are less predictable and often lead to richer discussions.

I also consider complementary curiosities. The person who's an expert in something paired with someone who's genuinely curious about that topic. Your friend who's a wine enthusiast with your colleague who wants to learn about wine. Your neighbor who's into photography with your friend who's planning a big trip and wants to learn to take better pictures.

Life stage connections often work well too. People going through similar transitions (new parents, recent graduates, empty nesters, career changers) have natural conversation material even if their backgrounds are completely different. But be thoughtful about this: someone who just got divorced might not want to spend the evening with newlyweds talking about relationship bliss.

Travel experiences create excellent conversation opportunities, but be strategic about it. Don't invite five people who have all been to Paris unless they went at different times or for different reasons. But do invite people who have traveled to different places but with similar travel styles (adventure travelers, culture seekers, food tourists).

Here's an advanced technique: seed conversations by sharing relevant information when you introduce people. Instead of "Marcus, meet Elena," try "Marcus, Elena just got back from that photography workshop in Iceland you were asking about." This gives them specific content to discuss and shows that you pay attention to what people care about.

I also seed conversations by sharing interesting details about guests in my invitations. "I'm looking forward to introducing you to my friend David who just started that urban beekeeping project" or "You'll love meeting Elena, she has the best stories about teaching English in rural Japan." This primes people to ask questions and shows genuine interest in supporting connections.

## Managing Different Social Energy Levels

One of the trickiest aspects of guest list planning is balancing different social energy levels and needs. Your naturally extroverted friends need different things from a party than your fellow introverts, and creating an environment where everyone feels comfortable requires careful consideration.

The mistake most people make is assuming that mixing personality types will naturally balance out. That extroverts will draw out introverts, and introverts will provide depth for extroverts. Sometimes this works, but often it just creates two different parties happening in the same space, with the extroverts dominating conversation while the introverts retreat to the edges.

Instead, I aim for compatible energy mixing. This means including people with different social styles who complement rather than compete with each other. The extrovert who loves asking questions paired with introverts who have interesting answers. The naturally social person who enjoys supporting conversation paired with people who appreciate being drawn into discussions rather than having to initiate them.

I also consider social stamina when planning timing and activities. If half your guests are likely to be ready to leave after two hours while the other half are just getting warmed up, plan your party structure accordingly. Create natural transition points where the early departures can leave gracefully without ending the party for people who want to stay longer.

Physical space planning matters for mixed energy groups too. Create both group conversation areas and smaller, quieter spaces where introverts can have more intimate discussions or take breaks from group interaction. This might mean setting up the living room for group conversation while keeping the kitchen available for smaller clusters, or creating a quiet corner with comfortable seating away from the main party area.

Activity planning should accommodate different comfort levels with group participation. Choose activities where people can engage at their own level rather than activities that require everyone to participate equally. A group cooking project lets some people take leadership roles while others contribute more quietly. Background music allows for both group conversation and smaller side discussions.

I've learned to give guests advance information about the social structure they can expect. "This will be a small group of six people, mostly folks from my hiking group" sets different expectations than "Come meet a mix of people from different parts of my life." This helps both introverts and extroverts calibrate their energy and expectations appropriately.

## The Art of Strategic Exclusion

This is the part of guest list planning that nobody wants to talk about: sometimes the best thing you can do for your party is not invite certain people. This doesn't make you a bad friend or a social gatekeeper. It makes you a thoughtful host who understands that every guest affects the experience for everyone else.

I've identified several types of people who consistently make parties more challenging for introvert hosts, not because they're bad people, but because they require management that drains hosting energy or disrupts group dynamics in ways that are hard to recover from.

The Conversation Dominator monopolizes group discussions and doesn't leave space for others to contribute. They're often intelligent and entertaining, but they turn gatherings into performance venues rather than conversation opportunities. In small groups especially, one dominant talker can prevent anyone else from being heard.

The Emotional Monopolizer brings heavy personal drama to social gatherings and expects the group to provide therapy and support. Again, not a bad person, but someone going through a crisis needs more focused attention than a party can provide. Save the one-on-one support for actual one-on-one time.

The Social Competitor treats every gathering like a networking opportunity or status competition. They're more interested in impressing people than connecting with them, and they can make other guests feel like they're being evaluated rather than enjoyed.

The Energy Vampire complains constantly, brings negative energy to every interaction, or creates interpersonal drama wherever they go. Some people consistently leave others feeling drained rather than energized, and that effect is amplified in small group settings.

The Wildcard is unpredictable in ways that create hosting anxiety. Maybe they drink too much sometimes, or they have strong political opinions they can't keep to themselves, or they've been known to create romantic drama at social gatherings. You find yourself spending mental energy managing potential problems instead of enjoying your own party.

Strategic exclusion doesn't mean cutting these people out of your life. It means being selective about which settings you include them in. The conversation dominator might be delightful one-on-one. The person in crisis might benefit more from actual one-on-one support than from party inclusion.

Consider not just whether you like someone, but whether their presence will enhance or complicate the evening for your other guests. Your shy friend won't bloom if someone's going to talk over them all night. Your colleague won't decompress if you've also invited the person who'll spend the evening listing their own grievances.

If you're already running low on hosting energy, this is not the time to invite the guest who requires the most management. Save them for when you have more to give.

# Budget Planning: The Introvert's Detailed Approach

Nobody who has ever stood in a grocery store at 4 PM on the day of their own party, holding a wheel of brie they didn't plan to buy, mentally calculating whether they can still afford wine, has ever said 'I'm really glad I didn't plan this earlier.' This chapter is for those of us who prefer to sort out the money stress before the party, not during it.

Let me tell you about the party that taught me why introverts need a completely different approach to party budgeting. I was hosting a housewarming and decided to "keep it simple", you know, just get some snacks, drinks, and decorations the day before. How hard could it be?

Cut to me at 2 PM the day of the party, standing in the grocery store having a full anxiety attack because I couldn't find the specific cheese I wanted, the bakery was out of the dessert I'd planned on, and I was doing frantic mental math trying to figure out if I had enough money left for wine after buying emergency replacement appetizers. I ended up spending twice my intended budget on a random collection of expensive items that didn't go together, all while my social battery drained from dealing with crowded stores and making rapid-fire decisions under pressure.

## Using Your Natural Planning Skills to Avoid Last-Minute Stress

Most people approach party budgeting the way they approach party planning: wing it and hope for the best. For introverts, this is genuinely terrible. Financial uncertainty on top of social uncertainty is a lot. The fix is spreading your budget decisions across three stages so you're never making expensive choices under pressure.

Three to four weeks out: set your total budget and break it into categories. For a dinner party of 8, I use roughly food (40%), drinks (30%), supplies (10%), decorations (10%), contingency (10%). The percentages are less important than having categories at all; they stop you from accidentally spending your entire food budget on a really good cheese situation and having nothing left for wine.

Two to three weeks out: research actual costs. Check grocery store prices online. If you're ordering anything, call ahead. This is when you find out your original menu was $40 over budget and swap the sea bass for the pasta dish you were considering anyway.

One week out through party day: execute the plan. By this point the hard decisions are already made. You're following a list, not improvising in a crowded store while your social battery drains in real time.

I keep a simple spreadsheet: planned cost, actual cost, running total. Not because I love spreadsheets, but because seeing that I'm on track is worth far more than the two minutes it takes to update.

The voice that says real hosts don't need a spreadsheet for a dinner party has also never done emergency mental math in a grocery store parking lot trying to figure out if they can still afford wine. The spreadsheet is not obsessive. The parking lot math is obsessive.

## Cost-Effective Solutions That Look Intentional, Not Cheap

Here's the truth about party budgets: your guests will never know how much you spent, but they will notice whether your choices feel thoughtful and cohesive. A $30 party that feels carefully planned will impress people more than a $100 party that feels thrown together.

What actually works is picking one clear direction and buying toward it. Not the cheapest thing, not the most impressive thing; just things that belong together. A cohesive $40 spread looks more intentional than a scattered $100 one.

Start with a simple theme or color palette, not because you're trying to be Pinterest-perfect, but because it helps you make consistent choices that look deliberate. "Cozy autumn dinner" gives you direction for food (hearty, seasonal), drinks (warm cocktails, red wine), and simple decorations (candles, small pumpkins). "Casual summer gathering" suggests lighter food, refreshing drinks, and outdoor-friendly setup.

For food, focus on dishes that look impressive but use affordable ingredients. A big pot of really good soup with artisanal bread feels more special than expensive appetizers that disappear in minutes. Pasta dishes can feed a crowd affordably while still feeling sophisticated if you choose interesting ingredients and present them well.

I've discovered that homemade food almost always feels more special than store-bought, even when it costs less. A simple cheese plate with good crackers, some fruit, and homemade jam feels more thoughtful than expensive pre-made appetizers. Cocktails mixed from basic spirits with fresh ingredients feel more special than premium alcohol served neat.

The presentation multiplier is real. Simple food served on actual plates with cloth napkins feels more elegant than expensive food on paper plates. Flowers from the grocery store in a nice vase look more intentional than elaborate decorations that obviously came from a party store.

Here's my favorite budget hack: the signature element. Choose one thing to spend a little extra money on that will anchor the whole experience. Maybe it's really good wine, or fresh flowers, or an excellent dessert, or high-quality coffee for after dinner. Having one elevated element makes everything else feel special by association.

For decorations, less is more when you're on a budget. A few candles create better ambiance than elaborate decorations, and they're reusable. String lights work for almost any occasion and cost very little. Fresh herbs or branches from your yard (or a friend's yard) make beautiful, free centerpieces.

The key is making choices that reinforce each other rather than pulling in different directions. A rustic dinner with homemade bread, simple wine, and candlelight feels cohesive and special. The same menu with fancy cocktails and elaborate decorations would feel confused and probably cost three times as much.

## Shopping Strategies That Minimize Social Interaction When Needed

Let's acknowledge something that most party planning advice completely ignores: shopping for parties can be socially exhausting for introverts. Crowded stores, pushy salespeople, having to ask where things are located, dealing with checkout lines when you're already stressed about hosting; it all adds up to significant energy drain before your party even starts.

I've developed shopping strategies that minimize social friction and preserve energy for the actual hosting. The goal is to make purchasing as smooth and predictable as possible.

Online ordering is your best friend when available. Grocery pickup or delivery eliminates store crowds and impulse purchases. You can shop at your own pace, compare prices easily, and stick to your list without distractions. Many stores let you reorder previous purchases, which is perfect for repeat items like wine or basic supplies.

For items you need to select personally (fresh produce, flowers, specialty foods), I've learned to shop at off-peak times and specific locations. Early morning or late evening grocery runs avoid crowds and rushed energy. Smaller, local markets often have more knowledgeable staff and less overwhelming environments than big chain stores.

I also batch my shopping strategically. Non-perishable items get purchased weeks ahead when I have energy and time to deal with stores. Perishable items get purchased 1-2 days before, when I know exactly what I need and can get in and out quickly. Last-minute items (ice, fresh herbs, forgotten essentials) come from smaller, less overwhelming stores when possible.

Create detailed shopping lists organized by store layout to minimize wandering around asking for help. Many grocery stores have store maps online, or you can create your own mental map during a low-pressure shopping trip. Group items by location: produce section, dairy, pantry items, frozen. This reduces time in store and eliminates the social interaction of asking where things are.

For specialty items or expensive purchases (wine, quality ingredients, serving pieces), research online first. Know exactly what you want and where to find it before you go to the store. This prevents the social pressure of having sales staff "help" you when you just need time to think and compare options.

Cash versus card strategies can reduce checkout anxiety too. If you're worried about staying on budget, bring cash for discretionary purchases. You can't overspend, and you don't have to do mental math about remaining balances. For planned purchases, card payments with budget tracking apps help you stay on track without cash-handling stress.

I also keep backup purchasing options for high-anxiety shopping days. If the store is too crowded or you're feeling overwhelmed, have a simplified backup plan. Know which items are essential versus nice-to-have. Identify alternative stores that might be less overwhelming. Don't force yourself through a terrible shopping experience for the sake of your original plan.

## Tracking Expenses to Maintain Control and Reduce Anxiety

Budget uncertainty is often more stressful than actual budget limitations. Not knowing whether you can afford the next item on your list creates low-level anxiety that stacks on top of everything else. The solution is visibility, knowing exactly where you stand at any point.

I use a simple traffic light in my head: green (under 70% spent, essentials covered, relax), yellow (70-90%, stick to the plan), red (90%+ or over in any single category, time to adjust). You can track this in a phone note with running totals. It takes thirty seconds after each purchase.

Track by category, not just total. Being under budget overall doesn't help if you've spent your entire food budget on appetizers and still need a main course. Keep separate limits for food, drinks, supplies, and decorations.

Build in a buffer. If your food budget is $80, plan as if it's $70. The $10 slack absorbs the thing you forgot to buy and the item that costs slightly more than the website said. It prevents the particular panic of being $7 over budget on something essential.

After each party, note what cost more than expected and what you'd skip next time. A dinner for eight probably costs less than you remember and more than you planned. Knowing the actual number makes the next one easier to budget from the start.

## Creating Financial Templates for Different Party Types

Once you've hosted a few parties and tracked your spending, you can create budget templates that make future planning much faster and more accurate. Instead of starting from scratch each time, you have proven frameworks that you can adjust based on guest count and specific needs.

I maintain templates for my most common party types: casual dinner for 6-8 people ($60-80), larger casual gathering for 10-12 ($100-120), special occasion dinner for 6-8 ($120-150), and holiday entertaining for 12-15 ($150-200). These ranges include everything except alcohol, which I budget separately based on my guests' preferences.

Each template includes typical costs for main categories, sample menus with grocery lists, and notes about what worked well or poorly. When I'm planning a dinner party, I can pull up my template, adjust for current prices and guest count, and have a solid budget framework in 15 minutes rather than starting from zero.

The first time I used a template instead of building a budget from scratch, I finished the whole thing in eleven minutes. I remember checking the clock because I couldn't believe it. The previous party had taken me two anxious hours of spreadsheet math to plan. Eleven minutes. Templates are not obsessive. Templates are freedom.

I also track cost-per-person for different types of gatherings. Casual dinners run about $10-12 per person for food. More elaborate dinners with appetizers and dessert run $15-20 per person. Cocktail parties with substantial appetizers run $12-15 per person. Having these benchmarks helps me quickly estimate costs for different guest counts.

Seasonal adjustments matter too. Summer parties often cost less because of fresh, affordable produce and outdoor eating. Winter parties cost more because of heartier food and more elaborate indoor setup. Holiday parties cost more because of special ingredients and decorations. These patterns, once built into your templates, make planning more realistic.

The templates also include timing guides for purchases. Certain items go on sale predictably (wine during holiday seasons, grilling supplies in summer, baking ingredients before holidays). Planning purchases around these cycles can significantly reduce costs without compromising quality.

Don't forget to include hidden costs in your templates: ice, extra napkins, replacement candles, emergency backup snacks. These small items add up and can blow your budget if you don't account for them. Including a "miscellaneous supplies" category prevents surprise expenses.

Update your templates after each party with actual costs and notes about what you'd change. Did the amount of food work out right? Was the wine adequate or did you run short? Did you buy too many decorations? This ongoing refinement makes each template more accurate and useful.

The investment in creating good budget templates pays off quickly. Party planning becomes faster and less stressful when you have proven frameworks rather than inventing everything from scratch. You'll also make better financial decisions because you're working from data rather than guesswork.

Your natural introvert planning skills are perfect for party budgeting. You think ahead, you consider details, you like having control over important decisions. These same qualities that might make you anxious about social situations can make you incredibly effective at creating memorable gatherings that don't break the bank or break your sanity.

# Food and Drink Mastery

Here's the honest truth about food at parties: guests will remember if it was terrible, forget if it was adequate, and occasionally remember if it was exceptional. What they'll definitely remember is whether they felt comfortable and welcome. So let's make food that's good enough to be memorable without turning you into a short-order cook in your own home.

I'll never forget the dinner party where I learned that knowing your audience isn't just about conversation topics; it's about understanding what people want to eat. I had invited a mix of friends from different parts of my life: my book club, my brother's gaming buddies, and a few colleagues from work.

I spent three days making an elaborate Mediterranean menu with quinoa-stuffed vegetables, homemade hummus, and a complex fish dish I'd found in a fancy cookbook. The book club friends were impressed. The work colleagues took photos. And the gaming guys ate politely while clearly wondering where the actual food was. By the end of the night, they were ordering pizza on their phones.

## Menu Planning for Different Party Sizes and Guest Types

I spent years making food I thought was impressive. The gaming guys ordering pizza at the end of my Mediterranean dinner cured me of that. Now I ask a simpler question: what do these specific people actually want to eat?

Small dinner parties (4-6 people) can handle more complex menus because you can manage detailed cooking while still being present with guests. This is where you can try that interesting recipe you've been wanting to attempt or create a cohesive dining experience with multiple courses. You can also accommodate specific dietary restrictions more easily when you're cooking for fewer people.

But here's what changes as group size increases: your ability to manage complex cooking decreases dramatically, while the need for food that travels well and stays good at room temperature increases. For parties of 8-12 people, you need dishes that can mostly be prepared ahead and require minimal last-minute attention.

The guest demographics matter as much as the numbers. When I host my hiking group after a long training weekend, I plan for people who've burned serious calories and want substantial, satisfying food. Think hearty chili, loaded nachos, thick sandwiches, pasta salads with actual protein. These aren't people who want to nibble on delicate appetizers; they want food that feels like fuel.

My book club gatherings call for lighter fare that supports conversation rather than dominating it. Small plates that can be eaten while talking, interesting cheeses with good bread, soups that can simmer while we discuss the book. The food should be good enough to comment on but not so complex that it becomes the focus of the evening.

Mixed professional groups need food that's substantial enough for people coming from work but sophisticated enough for colleagues who are used to business dining. This usually means elevated comfort food: really good versions of familiar dishes rather than exotic experiments.

Sports viewing parties have completely different requirements: food that can be eaten while standing, won't create mess during exciting moments, and provides steady fuel for several hours of sustained attention to the game. Finger foods, substantial dips, sliders, wings: things that don't require utensils or careful attention to consume.

Gaming groups (board games, video games, D&D sessions) need food that won't damage equipment, can be consumed one-handed, and provides sustained energy for long sessions. Think individual portions, minimal crumbs, easy-to-grab snacks that don't require stopping the activity.

I've learned to ask myself three questions when planning menus: What time of day will people be hungry? What level of hunger are they likely to have? What eating style fits the activity we're doing? A brunch gathering for runners who just finished a long training run requires very different food than an evening wine tasting with colleagues.

## Dietary Restrictions and Inclusive Options (Without Stress)

Dietary restrictions used to send me into planning spirals. How do you accommodate the vegetarian, the person avoiding gluten, the friend who's doing keto, and the colleague with severe nut allergies without cooking four different meals or making everyone feel weird about their food choices?

What I've stopped doing is trying to modify a standard menu to fit everyone's restrictions. It's exhausting and the workarounds usually show. Instead, I build the menu from dishes that are naturally inclusive, the kind that don't require a separate conversation to explain.

Start with naturally inclusive base foods: rice and quinoa work for almost everyone. Roasted vegetables are vegetarian, vegan, gluten-free, and generally healthy. Simple proteins like grilled chicken or fish can anchor a meal while leaving room for people to customize their plates.

Build-your-own setups are perfect for managing multiple dietary needs without multiplying your workload. Taco bars let people customize based on their restrictions, corn tortillas for gluten-free guests, beans for vegetarians, multiple protein options for different preferences. Salad bars with various toppings, pasta stations with different sauces, or grain bowls with mix-and-match components all follow the same principle.

Here's my practical system for managing restrictions without stress: When sending invitations, include a simple line asking about dietary restrictions or food allergies. Not preferences, not detailed nutrition plans, just restrictions that affect safety or basic ability to eat what you're serving.

Create a master list of ingredients for each dish you're planning. This lets you quickly answer questions about specific allergens or dietary concerns without having to remember every component. Keep this list accessible during the party for guests who want to check ingredients themselves.

Plan one "safe" dish that works for most common restrictions: a substantial salad with protein, a vegetable-based soup, a grain bowl with various toppings. This ensures that everyone has at least one filling option without requiring separate meal preparation.

Label dishes clearly but subtly. Small cards with dish names and basic dietary information (vegetarian, contains nuts, gluten-free) help people make choices without having to ask detailed questions about every item.

## Bar Setup and Beverage Calculations That Work

Beverage planning is where many introvert hosts either drastically overspend or run embarrassingly short, because most advice either assumes you're throwing college parties or formal cocktail events. Real parties with real people require much more nuanced planning based on your specific guests and timing.

The standard "one drink per person per hour" calculation is useless because it doesn't account for the huge variations in how different groups consume alcohol. My hiking group, especially after long outdoor activities, drinks significantly more than my book club. Gaming groups tend to nurse drinks slowly over several hours. Professional networking events require different calculations than casual friend gatherings.

Here's my realistic calculation system based on actual guest behavior patterns: For wine-focused groups (book clubs, dinner parties, sophisticated gatherings), plan 3-4 glasses per person over 3-4 hours. For beer-focused groups (sports viewing, casual hangouts, younger crowds), plan 2-3 beers per person for 3-4 hours. For mixed groups or cocktail-style parties, plan 2-3 drinks per person but include substantial non-alcoholic options.

The timing of consumption matters more than total quantity. Sports viewing parties see heavy drinking during exciting moments and halftime, with lighter consumption during focused game time. Dinner parties typically involve wine with dinner but lighter drinking before and after. Understanding these patterns helps you manage supply and serving logistics.

Non-alcoholic options require as much planning as alcoholic ones, especially since many people are reducing alcohol consumption for health, medication, or personal reasons. Stock interesting sodas, sparkling water with fruit, good coffee or tea options, and substantial beverages that feel special rather than default.

Bar setup affects consumption patterns and your hosting workload. Self-service bars work well for casual groups and reduce your serving duties, but require hardy glassware and spill-resistant setup. Cocktail service from you as host gives more control over consumption and timing but requires more of your attention during the party.

I've learned to create beverage stations that match the party flow and energy level. For active, standing parties, place drinks in multiple locations to prevent bottlenecks. For seated dinner parties, focus beverage service around the dining area. For long gaming sessions, create easily accessible drink stations that don't interfere with game setup.

Calculate backwards from your serving style: if you're opening wine throughout the evening, you need different quantities than if you're setting out beer for self-service. If you're making cocktails to order, you can control portions and timing. If drinks are self-serve, people will consume more and you need buffer quantities.

The voice that says you're overthinking the drinks: you're not. Running out of wine during dinner is a social event nobody forgets and everyone tells other people about. Think it through once so you never have to think about it again.

Consider the practical limitations of your space and equipment. If you only have 12 wine glasses, plan accordingly rather than assuming people will wash and reuse glasses during the party. If your refrigerator space is limited, factor that into your beer and white wine calculations.

## Make-Ahead Strategies and Timing for Different Cooking Levels

The difference between enjoying your own party and spending it frantically cooking in the kitchen comes down to understanding your actual cooking capacity and planning within it. This isn't about cooking skill level; it's about honest assessment of how much active food preparation you can handle while hosting.

Food works when it matches what people are actually there to do. Standing-and-talking parties need food you can eat with one hand without requiring a plate. Seated dinners can handle something more involved. Activity-focused gatherings, games, sports, anything where eating is secondary, need food that doesn't interrupt. The question isn't what category of person your guests are. It's what they'll be doing with their hands and attention while they eat.

Three questions that settle most menu decisions: What time of day will people be hungry, and how hungry? What are they doing while eating, and does the food support that? Is there anything on this table that a guest can't eat, and have I handled it? Answer those three and the menu mostly plans itself.

Food satisfaction comes from matching expectations and practical needs, not from objective food quality alone. A perfectly prepared quinoa salad will disappoint guests expecting substantial comfort food, while excellent wings might feel inappropriate for a sophisticated wine tasting.

# Entertainment That Works for Everyone

Entertainment at a party works like good background music: when it's right, nobody notices it and everything flows. When it's wrong, it's the only thing anyone can think about. This chapter will help you stop thinking of yourself as the entertainment and start thinking of yourself as the person who creates the conditions for entertainment to happen.

The most exhausting party I ever hosted was also the quietest. I had invited eight people for dinner, planned a beautiful meal, set up my space perfectly, and then realized around the appetizer course that I had no idea how to get people talking to each other. Three of my guests were meeting for the first time, two others barely knew anyone, and everyone was being politely conversational while waiting for someone else to create actual energy.

I spent the entire evening frantically trying to facilitate introductions, ask engaging questions, and somehow transform eight individual conversations into group connection. By dessert, I was socially exhausted from being the entertainment director, while my guests were being perfectly pleasant but not really engaging with each other.

## Structured Activities That Break the Ice Naturally

The problem with most icebreaker activities is that they feel forced and put people on the spot, which is especially uncomfortable for introverts. The solution is what I think of as stealth icebreakers: activities that create natural conversation opportunities without announcing themselves as team-building exercises.

Collaborative creation activities work brilliantly because they give people something to focus on besides the social pressure of making conversation. Setting up a build-your-own taco bar doesn't just solve dinner logistics; it creates natural interactions as people help each other reach ingredients, share topping preferences, and laugh about overloaded tortillas.

I've discovered that when people work together on simple tasks, conversations develop organically around the activity. The shared focus reduces social anxiety while providing natural talking points. Building individual pizzas, assembling fancy coffee drinks, or creating simple craft projects all follow this principle.

Memory-sharing activities tap into people's natural love of storytelling without putting anyone on the spot for original material. Setting out photo albums from shared experiences (if your guests know each other from somewhere specific) gives people concrete things to discuss. Travel photos, local hiking spots, or pictures from previous gatherings all work well.

For groups that don't share history, I use simple experience prompts: questions that invite storytelling but don't require personal revelation. "What's the most interesting place you've been this year?" or "What's something you learned recently that surprised you?" These prompts work because everyone has answers, but the responses reveal personality and create conversation hooks.

The best icebreakers don't feel like icebreakers. They feel like natural parts of the gathering that happen to create opportunities for connection. When people are focused on the activity rather than the social performance, genuine interactions develop much more easily.

I've learned to time icebreaking activities for maximum effectiveness. Right after arrival, people are often still settling in and not ready for structured interaction. But after 30-45 minutes, when initial greetings are done and people have had time to get comfortable, introducing a collaborative activity can shift the energy toward deeper engagement.

## Background Music That Fills Awkward Silences (Without Competing for Attention)

Music is one thing I offload whenever I can. At my bigger gatherings I hired a DJ or brought in a live band, belly dancers, folk musicians, people from the communities I was already part of. At smaller ones I put a playlist on and forgot about it. Both approaches work. What doesn't work is trying to manage music mid-party, adjusting songs while also trying to host. That's too many things at once.

If you're doing a playlist: build it in advance, set the volume before guests arrive, and leave it alone. The goal is a room that feels inhabited, not a room that sounds like a nightclub or a library. Interesting enough to notice, quiet enough to talk over.

If you're hiring a DJ or band: brief them. Tell them what the gathering is, who's coming, what you want the energy to feel like at different points. A good DJ reads the room and adjusts, but they need somewhere to start. A live band changes the atmosphere in a way no playlist can. If it's in your budget and fits your crowd, it's worth it.

## Games and Conversation Starters for Mixed Personality Types

The challenge with mixed groups is that no single activity appeals to everyone's comfort level and participation style. Competitive games intimidate some people while boring others. Deep conversation starters overwhelm some guests while feeling too superficial for others. The solution is layered entertainment that provides multiple ways to engage.

The key is optional participation design: setting up activities where people can engage at their own comfort level without feeling excluded if they prefer to observe. A simple puzzle on a side table lets some people work while others just talk nearby. Art supplies and blank paper invite creativity from people who enjoy it while providing conversation topics for people who prefer to comment rather than create.

Conversation starters work best when they're available but not mandatory. I create question jars with interesting prompts that people can use if conversation lags, but I don't force group discussions around them. "What's the strangest thing that happened to you this week?" or "If you could have dinner with anyone, living or dead, who would it be and why?" provide material for people who want it without pressuring anyone to participate.

Board games require careful selection for mixed groups. Avoid anything too competitive, too complex, or requiring specific cultural knowledge. Look for games that encourage storytelling, creativity, or collaboration rather than direct competition. Games that allow for side conversations during play work better than games requiring intense concentration.

The key is having multiple entertainment options available simultaneously rather than forcing the entire group into one activity. Some people can work on the puzzle while others play a card game while still others continue dinner conversation. This reduces pressure on any individual activity to entertain everyone.

Different personality types need different engagement strategies. Introverts often prefer activities they can ease into rather than jump into immediately. Extroverts might need higher-energy options to feel engaged. Competitive people appreciate games with clear objectives and rules. Creative people enjoy open-ended activities that allow for personal expression.

I've learned to read group energy and adjust entertainment offerings accordingly. If conversation is flowing naturally, I don't interrupt with organized activities. If energy is lagging or people seem stuck in small subgroups, introducing a group activity can help redistribute social energy.

# Managing Energy Levels Without Being the Constant Entertainer

I used to think that if the party energy flagged, it was on me to fix it. I'd jump in with a question, a game, a joke, anything to restart the engine. What I eventually figured out: most of the time I didn't need to do anything. The energy was fine. I was anxious.

The first step is understanding natural energy patterns in social gatherings. Most parties follow predictable energy curves: higher energy during arrival as people settle in, plateau during main activities, potential dip during transitions, and either sustained energy or gradual wind-down depending on timing and group composition.

Instead of fighting these patterns, design your party structure to work with them. Plan more active or engaging activities during natural high-energy periods. Use natural low-energy moments for transitions between activities or for people to step back and recharge. Don't try to maintain constant high energy throughout the entire event.

I've developed a seeding approach: introducing elements that generate ongoing engagement without requiring constant management from me. A collaborative playlist where people can add songs throughout the evening creates ongoing activity. Photo-taking opportunities give people reasons to interact with each other. Simple group projects that develop throughout the party provide sustained focus.

Recruiting natural facilitators from your guest list is one of the most effective energy management strategies. Most groups include people who enjoy social facilitation and are good at drawing others into conversation. Identify these people early and give them subtle opportunities to exercise these skills.

This doesn't mean asking people to co-host or making formal announcements. It means introducing the naturally social person to the shy person you want to help feel included. It means asking the storyteller to share an interesting experience you know will engage the group. It means positioning people with complementary interests where they can discover their commonalities naturally.

I once spent an entire party essentially doing nothing as a host because I'd invited the right mix of people and set up the space well. I kept waiting for something to go wrong. Nothing did. That was the night I understood what good hosting actually looks like from the outside: invisible.

I've learned to identify and use these natural conversation magnets rather than trying to impose entertainment from outside the group's interests. When people are talking about things they genuinely care about, they entertain each other much more effectively than any organized activity could.

The thing I've learned about activity design is that less structure is almost always better than more. The urge to plan entertainment from beginning to end is an anxiety response, not a hosting strategy. Guests don't need a program. They need permission and a starting point.

For mixed groups you don't know well: one optional activity, available but not announced. A puzzle on a side table. A question jar. A photo album. Something people can gravitate toward naturally when they want to.

For groups with a shared interest: one activity that lets them express it. My Star Trek friends didn't need entertainment, they needed a reason to argue about Federation policy. I provided that reason by putting on the wrong episode deliberately. An hour of passionate debate followed. My job was done in approximately thirty seconds.

The mistake is designing activities for the group you imagine rather than the group in front of you. I've set up elaborate games that nobody touched because the conversation was already too good to interrupt. I've had parties where a single unexpected object, a weird map, a stack of postcards, a book someone hadn't seen, generated two hours of unprompted discussion. Read the room. If it's working, don't fix it.

One backup activity is enough. Two is fine. More than that and you're managing a program instead of hosting a party.

## Environmental Entertainment: Setting Up Spaces That Generate Interaction

Sometimes the best entertainment isn't an activity at all; it's thoughtful design of your physical space that naturally encourages interaction and engagement. This approach works particularly well for introvert hosts because it requires advance planning rather than ongoing facilitation.

Conversation pieces strategically placed around your space provide natural talking points without requiring organized activities. Interesting books, unique art pieces, plants, collections, or travel mementos all give people things to comment on and ask questions about. The key is choosing items that invite discussion rather than just admiration.

I've discovered that functional entertainment works better than decorative entertainment. A beautiful chess set that people can use generates more interaction than expensive art that people look at once. A bookshelf with interesting titles creates more conversation than elaborate decorations that don't invite participation.

Photo displays work particularly well for generating stories and connections. Not formal portrait galleries, but casual collections of interesting experiences, travel photos, local adventures, pictures with friends, or images from hobbies and interests. These give people concrete things to ask about and share related experiences around.

Interactive elements that don't require host facilitation can provide ongoing entertainment throughout the party. A simple guest book where people can write comments or draw pictures, a puzzle that people can work on intermittently, or art supplies available for casual use all create opportunities for engagement without requiring your attention.

Technology can support environmental entertainment if used thoughtfully. A collaborative playlist that people can add to throughout the evening creates ongoing interaction. A photo slideshow of local hikes or travel destinations provides conversation material. Streaming interesting documentary content on mute can provide visual interest and discussion topics.

The goal is creating discovery opportunities: things people can engage with at their own pace. Some guests will actively participate while others prefer to observe and comment, but everyone has access to engagement opportunities that don't require performance or putting themselves on the spot.

The single best party prop I ever put out was a stack of old travel postcards I'd picked up at an estate sale. Cost me four dollars. People spent an hour going through them, trading stories about places they'd been or wanted to go. I didn't plan that. I just put something interesting on the table and watched what happened.

# The Details That Reduce Social Friction

Nobody leaves a party saying 'the coaster placement was exceptional.' But they do feel, on some level, whether the space was welcoming, easy to move through, and thoughtfully arranged. This chapter is about the invisible work: the small decisions that add up to a feeling guests can't quite name but definitely notice.

The best compliment I ever received about hosting came from my friend Marcus after a casual dinner party: "I never had to wonder what I was supposed to be doing." At first, I thought he was damning me with faint praise; wasn't spontaneity supposed to be fun? But then I realized he'd identified exactly what I'd been trying to achieve: creating gatherings where people could relax and be themselves because they understood the framework.

## Invitations That Set Clear Expectations (Without Sounding Controlling)

Most party invitations create more anxiety than they resolve because they leave too many questions unanswered. "Come for dinner Saturday!" sounds casual and fun, but it doesn't tell people what time to arrive, when the gathering will end, what to wear, whether to bring anything, or even what kind of food to expect.

For introverts, both hosting and attending, this ambiguity creates stress. As a host, you spend time answering the same questions from multiple people. As a guest, you worry about arriving too early, staying too late, or showing up inappropriately dressed for the occasion.

I've developed invitations that provide more context without sounding rigid or overly formal. The key is framing details as helpful information rather than strict requirements.

Instead of "Come for dinner Saturday," try "Join us for casual dinner Saturday from 6-9 PM. I'm making that pasta dish you loved, and we'll eat around 7. Just bring yourselves!" This invitation tells people the time frame, sets expectations about formality level, gives a hint about food, and explicitly states they don't need to bring anything.

For different types of gatherings, the essential information changes but the principle remains the same: give people enough context to feel confident about their choices. Sports viewing parties need information about timing around game schedules. Professional gatherings need clarity about networking versus purely social expectations. Gaming sessions need information about duration and experience levels required.

I include context in my invitations: information that helps people mentally prepare for the social environment. "Small group of 6 people, mostly folks from my hiking group" sets different expectations than "Mix of people from different parts of my life." "Casual conversation over dinner" suggests different energy than "Game night with optional competitive elements."

The response mechanism matters as much as the invitation content. Make it easy for people to respond and ask questions without feeling high-maintenance. "Reply by Thursday if you can make it, text, email, or carrier pigeon all work!" gives people options and reduces the pressure of formal RSVP protocols.

I also include my contact information and explicitly invite questions: "Text me if you have any questions about timing, directions, or what to expect." This prevents people from feeling awkward about asking for clarification and reduces the number of day-of logistics questions you need to handle.

Different invitation formats work better for different communities and relationship contexts. Text invitations work well for casual friend groups and provide easy response mechanisms. Email invitations allow for more detailed information and work well for professional or mixed groups. Physical invitations signal special occasions and work well for milestone celebrations.

Clear communication reduces social anxiety for everyone, not just introverts. When people understand what's expected and what they can expect, they arrive more relaxed and ready to engage rather than spending mental energy decoding social signals.

## Thoughtful Touches That Show You Care Without Grand Gestures

The hosting advice industrial complex wants you to believe that memorable parties require elaborate themes, expensive decorations, and Instagram-worthy presentations. But the touches that make guests feel cared for are usually much simpler and more personal.

I've learned that thoughtful details work better than impressive displays because they show attention to your specific guests rather than generic hosting ambition. Remembering that Sarah always drinks tea instead of coffee and having good tea available means more than an elaborate coffee bar that doesn't serve her preferences.

The details I care most about are the ones nobody notices when they're right. Good lighting that makes everyone look flattering. Music at a volume where you don't have to raise your voice. A bathroom with good lighting and basic supplies. Coat storage that doesn't pile up in the hallway.

These details matter more than decorative elements because they affect people's actual comfort and ability to enjoy themselves. Someone struggling to find a place to set down their drink or wondering where to put their coat is not fully present for social interaction.

I focus on anticipatory thinking: working through the guest experience from arrival to departure and eliminating potential friction points. This might mean clearing sightlines so people can see conversation opportunities when they arrive, or ensuring there are multiple conversation areas so people aren't trapped in one group all evening.

The most effective thoughtful touches solve problems your guests didn't even realize they had. Having phone chargers easily available eliminates the anxiety of dying batteries. Providing small plates for appetizers prevents the awkward balancing act of trying to eat finger foods while holding drinks.

Creating clear sight lines to bathrooms eliminates the need to ask for directions.

I've discovered that personal touches matter more than expensive ones. Handwritten place cards for dinner parties, playlists that include songs you know specific guests enjoy, or small favors that relate to shared interests or experiences create much more meaningful impressions than generic luxury items.

## Memory-Making That Doesn't Require You to Be "On" All Night

Traditional party memory-making often puts enormous pressure on hosts to orchestrate special moments, take photos constantly, and ensure that everyone is having an Instagram-worthy experience. This approach is exhausting for introvert hosts who need to manage their own energy while supporting others' experiences.

The solution is designing memory-making opportunities that happen naturally throughout the event rather than requiring your constant attention and facilitation.

Simple photo opportunities work better than elaborate photo shoots. Setting up good lighting in conversation areas means candid photos will turn out well without requiring formal posing sessions. Having interesting backgrounds available, a bookshelf, artwork, or even just good window light, gives people natural settings for photos without staging requirements.

I've learned that the best party memories often come from genuine interactions rather than orchestrated activities. Creating comfortable conversation environments where people can share stories, discover commonalities, or have meaningful discussions often generates more lasting memories than elaborate entertainment programs.

Group projects that develop throughout the evening create natural documentation opportunities. A collaborative playlist where people add songs, a group photo album that people can contribute to throughout the party, or even a simple guest book where people can write comments all provide memory artifacts without requiring host orchestration.

Forced memory-making often feels artificial and pressured, while organic memory-making develops naturally when people are genuinely engaged and comfortable. Your job as host is to create environments where meaningful interactions can happen, not to personally document every moment.

I focus on passive memory collection: setting up systems that capture memories without requiring active management. Having a camera easily available for anyone to use, creating hashtags for social media sharing if your group uses social platforms, or simply ensuring good lighting throughout your space all support memory-making without demanding your constant attention.

## Graceful Party Endings That Work for Everyone

The most awkward part of many parties is the ending; nobody knows when it's appropriate to leave, hosts don't know how to signal wind-down time, and people end up staying longer than they wanted while hosts become increasingly exhausted. This is particularly challenging for introvert hosts who need to manage their own energy depletion while ensuring guests don't feel kicked out.

The solution is building party endings into the structure from the beginning rather than trying to manage them spontaneously when you're already socially depleted.

Time boundaries communicated in advance solve most ending problems before they start. When invitations specify "dinner from 6-9 PM" or "game night until around 11," people can plan their energy and departure timing accordingly. This also gives you permission to start wind-down activities around the specified end time.

Environmental cues work better than verbal announcements for signaling party transitions. Switching to quieter music, dimming lights slightly, serving coffee or tea instead of continuing alcohol service, or moving cleanup activities to visible areas all suggest natural wind-down without requiring awkward announcements.

I've developed exit permission strategies that give people easy opportunities without making them feel rude. Thanking people for coming when they start gathering their belongings, walking people to the door rather than letting them find their own way out, and explicitly stating that you understand people have different energy levels all help normalize leaving.

People leave when they're ready, and your job is to make that easy without making it awkward. Some guests have hard stops, childcare, early mornings, long drives. Others will stay as long as the conversation holds. Building a clear end time into your invitation handles most of this automatically: people who need to leave early have cover, and people who want to stay know when the host expects to wind down.

Good party endings leave everyone feeling satisfied rather than either cut off abruptly or trapped in a gathering that's lost momentum. People should leave feeling like they've had enough good conversation and connection, not like they're escaping or abandoning their host.

## Post-Party Follow-Up That Builds Relationships

The party doesn't really end when the last guest leaves; the follow-up period offers opportunities to strengthen connections and set foundations for future gatherings. But many hosts, especially introverts who are socially depleted after hosting, skip this crucial relationship-building opportunity.

I've developed simple follow-up systems that require minimal energy but create maximum relationship impact. The key is having systems in place so you can execute follow-up even when you're in post-party recovery mode.

Thank you messages work best when they're specific rather than generic. Instead of "Thanks for coming!" try "I loved hearing about your photography project, can't wait to see how it develops" or "That story about your hiking mishap had me laughing for hours." These messages show you were present and engaged during conversations.

Photo sharing creates ongoing connection opportunities if handled thoughtfully. Rather than dumping all party photos in a group message, curate a few good shots and share them with individual people or small groups. This gives you reasons to continue conversations and shows attention to people's interests and preferences.

Supporting connections can extend party relationships beyond the immediate gathering. If you introduced people who hit it off, following up to see if they've connected further shows thoughtful hosting. If someone mentioned looking for recommendations that another guest could provide, supporting that connection creates value for both people.

The timing of follow-up matters more than the elaborateness. Simple messages sent within a few days of the party feel natural and genuine. Follow-up that's delayed for weeks feels obligatory and loses connection to the original gathering.

I also use post-party follow-up to gather information that improves future hosting. Not formal surveys, but casual conversations about what people enjoyed, what worked well, and what they'd be interested in for future gatherings. This information helps you refine your hosting approach and plan events that better serve your community.

### Creating Systems That Support Consistent Hosting

The details that reduce social friction become much easier to manage when you develop standard systems rather than reinventing your approach for each gathering. I've created hosting templates that handle routine decisions and let me focus on what actually matters for each gathering.

Standard invitation templates for different types of gatherings eliminate the need to compose invitations from scratch each time. I have templates for casual dinners, game nights, professional gatherings, and special occasions that I can customize with specific details while maintaining consistent information and tone.

Supply checklists ensure I don't forget basic comfort elements that make gatherings run smoothly. Basic party supplies, backup serving pieces, emergency cleaning supplies, and guest comfort items all get included in my standard preparation process.

Setup routines help me create consistently comfortable environments without having to rethink space arrangement for each gathering. I know which furniture arrangements work well for different group sizes and activities, where to place lighting for best effect, and how to optimize traffic flow for my specific space.

The goal isn't to make every party identical, but to establish reliable systems that handle routine elements so you can focus creative energy on the aspects that matter most for your specific guests and occasion. When the logistics run smoothly, you have more capacity for the relationship-building and connection-supporting that make gatherings truly meaningful.

**The most instructive venue mistake I made was hosting a Renaissance festival gathering in my tiny studio apartment. Eight people in elaborate costumes, capes, swords, wide skirts, packed into 400 square feet. Nobody could move without knocking someone's prop. Conversations couldn't form because there was no space for people to arrange themselves. The party wasn't bad because of the food or the company. It was bad because the space fought everything we were trying to do.**

That disaster taught me that venue isn't just about having space for bodies. It's about creating an environment that supports the specific type of gathering you want, the personalities of your guests, and most importantly, your own comfort and energy management as the host. Your space choices affect everything from conversation flow to how much energy you'll spend managing logistics.

The default assumption is that hosting at home is always cheaper and easier than booking external venues. For introverts, that's not necessarily true. Sometimes the cost of transforming your space, managing all the logistics yourself, and dealing with cleanup afterward outweighs the rental cost of a venue that already works for your event.

I've developed a full-cost assessment for venue decisions. This goes beyond just financial costs to include time, energy, and stress factors that matter as much as money when you're planning within your introvert capacity.

## Home Parties vs. External Venues: The Real Cost-Benefit Analysis

Home venue advantages include complete control over the environment, no time limits or restrictions, familiar surroundings that reduce your baseline anxiety, ability to prepare food in your own kitchen with equipment you know, and obviously, no rental costs. You can set up exactly how you want, adjust lighting and music throughout the event, and retreat to private spaces when you need recharge breaks.

But home hosting also means you're responsible for everything: providing all furniture and serving pieces, managing temperature control and lighting, handling all cleanup during and after, dealing with noise considerations for neighbors, and working within whatever space limitations you have. Your home also might not naturally fit the type of gathering you want to create.

External venues make sense when your home doesn't support your vision, when the logistics of home hosting would overwhelm you, or when you want to create a special experience that requires specific facilities. Renting a small community center room for your board game group means everyone can spread out comfortably. Booking a private dining room for a special dinner means you can focus on conversation instead of serving logistics.

The hidden costs of external venues include not just rental fees, but transportation for supplies, less control over timing and setup, potential deposit requirements, and having to work within someone else's rules. You might also need to bring more supplies since you can't assume availability of basic items.

Here's my decision framework: If the event requires significant home modification (moving furniture, extensive decorating, unusual equipment), external venues often make sense. If your guest count pushes your space past comfortable capacity, look elsewhere. If the activity needs specific facilities (dance space, large kitchen, outdoor area), find a venue that provides what you need.

But if your home naturally supports your gathering type and guest count, the convenience and control usually outweigh the extra work. You just need to plan the space setup as carefully as you plan everything else.

## Space Flow and Traffic Patterns for Different Guest Types

Good space flow isn't just about having enough square footage. It's about understanding how different types of people move through and use space, and designing your setup to support natural interaction patterns while preventing bottlenecks and awkward clustering.

Different social groups have completely different space needs and movement patterns. When I host my hiking group, they naturally spread out and move around frequently, examining maps and gear, telling stories with gestures. They need open floor space and multiple conversation zones. When I host my book club, they prefer intimate seating where everyone can hear each other easily, with side tables for drinks and notebooks.

For mixed groups where you don't know everyone's preferences, create multiple zones with different space characteristics. Set up a formal conversation area with proper seating, a casual standing area around the kitchen or bar, and a quiet corner with comfortable chairs for people who want to step back from group energy.

Traffic flow matters more in smaller spaces where bottlenecks can kill conversation momentum. The classic mistake is putting all the food and drinks in one small area; everyone congregates there, making it impossible for anyone to access refreshments. Instead, distribute resources across multiple locations or create a logical flow that keeps people moving.

I've learned to trace the physical path guests will take through my space and eliminate friction points. Wide enough walkways between furniture, clear sight lines so people can see conversation opportunities, strategic placement of coats and bags so they don't create clutter in social areas.

The kitchen island has become my favorite space design element because it creates natural gathering opportunities while maintaining flow. People can help with food prep, grab drinks, or just lean and chat while others move around them. It's particularly good for introverts because you can participate in conversation while having a task to focus on.

## Lighting and Ambiance That Reduces Social Pressure

Lighting is the secret weapon of introvert hosts because it dramatically affects the social atmosphere without requiring any ongoing management from you. Good lighting makes everyone look better, feel more relaxed, and behave more naturally. Bad lighting creates stress that guests can't identify but definitely feel.

The biggest lighting mistake is relying entirely on overhead fixtures, which create harsh shadows and institutional feeling. Instead, use multiple light sources at different levels: table lamps, floor lamps, candles, string lights. This creates depth and warmth that makes spaces feel intimate and comfortable.

Dimmer switches are worth their weight in gold because they let you adjust energy throughout the event. Brighter lighting during arrival and food service helps people navigate and see each other clearly. Dimmed lighting during conversation periods creates intimacy and relaxation. You can subtly signal transitions by adjusting light levels.

Candles are magic for creating atmosphere, but use them strategically. Unscented candles prevent competing with food aromas. LED candles eliminate fire safety concerns and won't drip wax on your furniture. Group candles in clusters rather than spacing them evenly for more dramatic effect.

Different activities need different lighting approaches. Game nights need enough light for people to see cards and boards clearly, but not so bright that it feels like a classroom. Dinner parties benefit from warm, intimate lighting that encourages lingering conversation. Cocktail parties can handle more dramatic lighting with shadows and highlights.

I've learned to test my lighting setup before parties by sitting in different seats and checking sight lines. Can people see each other's faces clearly enough for conversation? Are there weird shadows or glare spots? Does the lighting feel appropriate for the mood you want to create?

Natural light timing matters too. Afternoon parties in spaces with large windows might need window coverings to prevent glare. Evening parties that extend past sunset need artificial lighting that maintains the same energy level as daylight fades.

Color temperature makes a bigger difference than most people realize. Warm light (lower color temperature) feels cozy and intimate, perfect for dinner parties and evening gatherings. Cooler light feels more energetic and alert, better for daytime events or active gatherings.

## Temperature, Acoustics, and Comfort Factors

The environmental factors that most people don't think about until something goes wrong can make or break a party, especially for introverts who are sensitive to sensory overload. Temperature, sound levels, air quality, and physical comfort directly affect your guests' ability to relax and enjoy themselves.

Temperature management is trickier than it seems because rooms with multiple people heat up quickly, but you can't make initial conditions uncomfortable for early arrivals. I've learned to start parties slightly cooler than normal comfortable temperature, knowing that body heat and kitchen activity will warm things up. Open windows or adjust air conditioning proactively rather than waiting for someone to complain.

Acoustics affect everything about conversation flow and energy management. Hard surfaces (tile, hardwood, large windows) create echo and amplify noise, making conversation more difficult as the party gets louder. Soft furnishings (rugs, curtains, upholstered furniture) absorb sound and create more intimate acoustic environments.

Music volume is the classic hosting challenge: too quiet and it feels awkward, too loud and people can't hear each other talk. The trick is starting quieter than feels right and gradually increasing volume as the party energy builds and ambient noise increases. People will naturally speak louder as the evening progresses, so the music needs to grow with them.

For groups with specific acoustic needs, plan accordingly. Musicians and music lovers are more sensitive to sound quality and might prefer no background music to poor-quality audio. Theater and performance communities might appreciate more dramatic acoustic environments. Sports groups are often comfortable with higher energy, louder environments.

Air quality matters more than most hosts realize, especially in smaller spaces with cooking happening. Kitchen fans, open windows, or air purifiers prevent stuffiness that makes people tired and cranky. Avoid competing scents from candles, air fresheners, and food preparation.

Seating comfort affects how long people want to stay and how much they participate in conversation. Mix seating types to accommodate different preferences and physical needs. Some people prefer firm chairs with back support, others like soft couches they can sink into. Floor seating works for some groups but not others.

I always make sure the basics are covered: accessible bathroom with good lighting, coat storage that doesn't pile up, somewhere for people to set down drinks, clear pathways.

## Creating Cozy Corners and Escape Routes

One of the most important but overlooked aspects of venue setup for introvert hosts is creating spaces where people can step back from group energy without leaving the party entirely. These "decompression zones" benefit both introverted guests who need breaks and you as the host when you need to recharge.

Cozy corners work best when they're visually connected to the main party space but acoustically separated enough for quieter conversation. A reading nook with comfortable chairs, a window seat with cushions, or even just two chairs positioned slightly away from the main group can provide this function.

These spaces need to feel intentional rather than accidental. Add a small side table, good lighting for conversation, maybe an interesting book or magazine. The goal is creating a legitimate reason for people to sit there rather than making it feel like exile from the main party.

I've learned that escape routes matter as much as gathering spaces. People need to be able to move to the bathroom, kitchen, or outside without disrupting ongoing conversations or drawing attention to themselves. This is especially important for introverted guests who might need frequent short breaks.

The host escape route is crucial for your own energy management. You need legitimate reasons to step away from hosting duties that don't make guests feel abandoned. Kitchen tasks, checking on outside areas, adjusting lighting or music: these activities give you brief solo time while appearing attentive to hosting responsibilities.

I also create optional tasks that let people step out of conversation when they need a break. Photo albums that people can flip through, a simple puzzle on a side table, interesting books or magazines in quiet areas. These give people something to do that looks social but doesn't require active participation.

# Pre-Party Preparation Systems

The goal of all pre-party preparation is simple: by the time your first guest rings the doorbell, you should be done. Not almost done. Not 'just finishing up.' Done. Calm. Possibly eating a snack and listening to the playlist you made. This chapter is about how to actually get there.

## Timeline Planning That Prevents Last-Minute Panic

The difference between confident hosting and stress hosting usually comes down to timeline management. When you're scrambling to finish food prep while guests are arriving, you can't be present for the social aspects of hosting that matter. When you're worried about whether you've forgotten something important, you can't relax and enjoy your own party.

I plan backwards from the moment guests arrive. Start there: when do you need to be dressed, calm, and done with all decisions? Work back from that point. Most people drastically underestimate how long the final hour of prep takes when they're also getting themselves ready and managing pre-party anxiety.

Two anchor points: when guests arrive and when food needs to be ready. Work backwards from both. Add 30 minutes of buffer to whatever you think you need, not because you'll use it, but because having it means you won't spiral when one thing takes longer than planned.

Working backwards from Guest Arrival: You need 30 minutes minimum for final setup, personal preparation, and mental transition from preparation mode to hosting mode. This means all major preparation tasks need to be complete 30 minutes before your stated start time, not when guests are supposed to arrive.

Working backwards from Food Service: Different types of meals require different advance timing. Simple meals (pasta, salads, sandwiches) can be finished the day of the party.

Complex meals (braises, baked dishes, elaborate desserts) need components finished 1-2 days in advance. Anything requiring precise timing (soufflés, fried foods, delicate sauces) should be avoided for hosting situations unless you're an experienced cook.

Here's my standard timeline template for dinner parties: Two weeks before, set date, send invitations, plan menu. One week before, grocery shop for non-perishables, confirm guest count, prepare any dishes that freeze well. Three days before, final grocery shopping, major prep cooking (sauces, desserts, anything that improves with time). Day before, final food prep, space setup, personal preparation. Day of, final touches, personal care, transition to hosting mode.

The first time I wrote this down instead of keeping it in my head, I realized I'd been routinely starting my day-of cooking three hours too late. Not because I'm bad at math. Because I'd never actually calculated it; I just hoped it would work out. It didn't, repeatedly. The template didn't make me faster. It made me honest.

Good timeline planning feels like having more time rather than less time. When tasks are properly distributed, nothing feels rushed or overwhelming. You have buffer time for things taking longer than expected, space for last-minute adjustments, and energy left for enjoying your own party.

## Delegation Strategies for Natural Collaborators

One of the biggest mistakes introvert hosts make is trying to handle every aspect of party preparation personally. We often assume that delegation creates more work (explaining what we want, coordinating with others, risking things not being done "right") than just doing everything ourselves. But strategic delegation reduces hosting stress while giving naturally helpful people ways to contribute meaningfully.

I've learned to be specific. "Can you help?" gets you someone standing in your kitchen asking what to do. "Could you arrive early and handle introductions while I finish cooking?" gets you actual help. My friend Erika is a natural facilitator; she's the one I call for that. My friend Marcus would rather carry things and assemble furniture than talk to strangers, so that's what I ask him to do.

Match the task to the person. Your most organized friend wants to handle logistics. Give them the shopping run or the setup checklist. Your socially gifted friend wants to manage people. Ask them to arrive early and handle introductions while you finish cooking. Your creative friend wants to contribute something aesthetic. Hand them the playlist or the flowers. People help better when the task matches what they actually enjoy doing.

The key is framing delegation as contribution opportunities rather than burden requests. Instead of 'Can you help me with my party?' try 'I'm planning a dinner party and thought you might enjoy creating the playlist. You always have great music recommendations.' This positions the request as recognition of their skills rather than as imposing on their time.

I've learned to delegate early in the planning process rather than waiting until I'm overwhelmed and desperate for help. When people have advance notice and clear parameters, they can contribute more thoughtfully and feel genuinely involved in the party's success rather than just helping with last-minute rescue operations.

## Contingency Planning for Your Peace of Mind

Introvert hosts often experience anxiety not just about things going wrong, but about not knowing what to do if things go wrong. The solution isn't to prevent all possible problems (impossible), but to have response plans for likely scenarios so you can handle issues calmly when they arise.

What actually helps is a simple scenario exercise: thinking through the most likely problems for each type of gathering and having a response ready. This isn't paranoid over-planning. It's having mental frameworks that reduce decision fatigue when you're already stressed.

Weather contingencies matter for any gathering with outdoor elements, but they also affect indoor parties more than people realize. Heavy rain might mean wet guests, muddy shoes, and different arrival patterns. Extreme heat might require additional cooling, different food safety considerations, and guest comfort adjustments.

For each party, I identify weather backup plans early in the planning process. Outdoor gatherings need complete indoor alternatives, including space arrangement, food service adjustments, and activity modifications. Indoor parties need strategies for dealing with weather-affected guest arrival, coat storage for wet items, and potential heating or cooling adjustments.

Food contingencies cover the most common hosting anxiety sources: dishes that don't turn out as expected, running out of food, or discovering last-minute dietary restrictions you didn't plan for. The solution is building buffer capacity into your menu planning rather than trying to predict exact needs.

I always plan 10-15% more food than mathematical calculations suggest, keep simple backup options available (good bread, cheese, fruit that can become an additional course), and maintain relationships with nearby restaurants that can provide emergency additions if needed. For drinks, I calculate generously and keep backup beverages that don't spoil if unused.

Guest contingencies address the social dynamics challenges that can derail parties: people who cancel last-minute, unexpected plus-ones, guests who arrive very early or very late, or personality conflicts that create uncomfortable situations. Having response strategies reduces the stress of handling these situations in the moment.

I've learned that most contingency planning involves having backup options rather than complex emergency procedures.

Keep extra supplies available, maintain flexible timing, know where to get last-minute additions, and have simplified alternatives for complex plans that might not work out.

The mental health benefit of contingency planning is often more valuable than the practical benefit. Knowing you have response strategies available reduces background anxiety and lets you focus on hosting rather than worrying about potential problems. When issues do arise, having plans available means you can respond calmly rather than panicking or feeling helpless.

The one contingency I now plan for without fail: what I will do if I'm overwhelmed mid-party and need five minutes alone. I know exactly where I'll go (kitchen), what I'll say ('just checking on things'), and how long I'll give myself. Having that exit rehearsed means I never have to improvise it in the moment, which is when it goes wrong.

The voice that says this level of preparation is excessive has never had to pivot an outdoor dinner party to a cramped kitchen while twelve people stood in the rain waiting for a decision. Plan for the rain.

## Energy Conservation Techniques for the Big Day

Party day energy management is crucial for introvert hosts because social hosting requires sustained mental and emotional energy that can't be easily replenished once depleted. The goal is entering party time with maximum available energy rather than arriving at your own gathering already exhausted from preparation.

Schedule the hard stuff for when you have energy and the easy stuff for when you don't. Grocery shopping requires decisions. Chopping vegetables doesn't. Setting the table is meditative. Planning the seating arrangement is not. I do the thinking-heavy tasks two days out and leave party day for execution only.

The biggest energy drain for most introvert hosts is decision-making under time pressure. When you're trying to decide what to wear, how to arrange flowers, and whether the food tastes right while guests are arriving, decision fatigue combines with social anxiety to create overwhelming stress.

The solution is front-loading as many decisions as possible to earlier in the week when you have more mental capacity. Choose your outfit and set it aside. Plan your final setup steps and write them down. Taste-test your menu components in advance so you know they work. This transforms party day from a series of decisions into a series of executions.

My party day rules are simple: no social commitments outside of party prep, easy food for myself (easy breakfast, light lunch that doesn't compete with party food), strategic use of caffeine if you normally consume it, and protection of alone time for mental preparation.

Physical energy conservation matters as much as mental energy conservation. Standing for long periods while cooking or setup can leave you physically tired before guests even arrive. I plan sitting breaks during preparation, use comfortable shoes during setup, and avoid physical tasks that aren't essential for party success.

Different types of gatherings require different energy management strategies based on their demands and timing. Evening dinner parties allow for afternoon rest time and gradual preparation throughout the day. Brunch gatherings require morning energy conservation and efficient preparation systems. All-day events need sustained energy management with planned recharge breaks.

## Creating Preparation Templates for Different Party Types

Once you've hosted several successful gatherings, you can create standardized preparation templates that eliminate the need to reinvent your planning process for each party. These templates handle routine decisions and timing so you can focus creative energy on elements that matter for your specific guests and occasion.

I maintain preparation templates for my most common party types: casual dinners for 6-8 people, larger casual gatherings for 10-12 people, special occasion dinners, holiday entertaining, and activity-focused gatherings like game nights or sports viewing. Each template includes timeline frameworks, shopping list templates, setup procedures, and energy management strategies.

The timeline templates provide tested frameworks for task distribution and scheduling. I know from experience that certain combinations of dishes require specific advance timing, that my space setup takes a predictable amount of time, and that I need consistent buffer periods for unexpected delays or complications.

Shopping list templates eliminate the mental work of remembering basic party supplies while ensuring I don't forget crucial elements. These lists include not just food and drinks, but hosting supplies, emergency backup items, and comfort elements that make parties run smoothly.

Setup procedure templates provide step-by-step processes for creating consistently comfortable environments. These include furniture arrangement, lighting optimization, supply placement, and traffic flow considerations that I've learned work well for my space and hosting style.

The goal isn't to make every party identical, but to establish reliable frameworks that handle routine elements efficiently. When the logistics are systematized, you have more mental capacity for the relationship-building and connection-supporting that make gatherings truly meaningful.

I update my templates after each party with notes about what worked well, what could be improved, and what might be adapted for different situations. This creates continuously improving systems that get more effective and less stressful over time.

# During the Party: Authentic Hosting

You planned, you prepped, you worried, and now they're here, actual people in your home, making noise, eating your food, requiring your presence. Here's the surprising part: this is actually the easy portion of the whole endeavor. If you've done the preparation work, your job now is mostly to show up as yourself and let the party run. Mostly.

The moment I stopped trying to be the perfect host was the moment I became a better one. It happened during a dinner party where I'd planned everything meticulously, the menu was flawless, the table looked magazine-worthy, and I had conversation topics prepared in case of awkward silences. But 30 minutes into the party, I realized I was performing hosting rather than hosting.

I was so focused on executing my hosting script that I wasn't really present with my guests. I was asking scripted questions instead of listening to actual answers. I was monitoring the evening for problems instead of enjoying the conversations happening around me. I was being the host I thought I should be instead of being myself with people I genuinely cared about.

That's when my friend David spilled red wine on my carefully set table, and instead of panicking about the stain, I found myself laughing about it with him while we cleaned it up together. That small moment of authentic response, treating a minor disaster as a funny story instead of a hosting failure, shifted the entire energy of the evening. People relaxed because I had relaxed, and the party became genuinely fun instead of carefully orchestrated.

## Being Genuinely Yourself Instead of Playing an Extroverted Role

The biggest hosting mistake introverts make is trying to impersonate extroverted hosts we've seen or read about. We think good hosting means being constantly "on," moving energetically between guests, maintaining high enthusiasm throughout the evening, and being the entertaining center of attention. But this performance is exhausting and ultimately ineffective because it's not sustainable or authentic.

Authentic introvert hosting looks completely different from extrovert hosting, and that's exactly why it works so well. Instead of being the energetic facilitator, you become the thoughtful observer who notices when someone needs inclusion or when conversations need gentle redirection. Instead of entertaining everyone personally, you create environments where people entertain each other.

I've learned that my natural introvert tendencies are hosting strengths when I stop trying to hide them. My preference for deeper conversations means I ask follow-up questions that help people share meaningful stories. My tendency to observe before acting means I notice social dynamics that need attention. My need for quieter moments means I create spaces where other introverts can recharge too.

Guests don't need you to be someone you're not; they need you to be fully present as yourself. When you're comfortable in your own hosting style, guests feel free to be comfortable in their own social styles too. This creates more authentic interactions than any amount of forced entertainment could achieve.

A few things tell me whether I'm actually hosting or just performing. I check in with my actual energy level rather than pushing through fatigue. I ask questions I'm genuinely curious about rather than questions I think I should ask. I share stories that interest me rather than trying to be universally entertaining.

The result is hosting that feels sustainable and genuine rather than draining and artificial. When you're being yourself, you have access to your natural social skills and instincts rather than trying to execute someone else's hosting playbook.

## Reading the Room and Making Subtle Adjustments

One of the most valuable introvert hosting skills is the ability to read social dynamics and make gentle course corrections without disrupting the natural flow of interaction. This requires the observational skills that introverts naturally possess, combined with strategic intervention techniques that work within your energy capacity.

What works for me is a quick temperature check throughout parties, regularly scanning the overall energy level, individual comfort levels, and group dynamics to identify areas that might need attention. This isn't constant monitoring that prevents you from enjoying yourself, but periodic awareness that helps you catch potential issues before they become problems.

Energy level assessment involves noticing whether the overall party energy matches the intended atmosphere and timing. Early in the evening, energy might be building as people arrive and settle in. Mid-party, energy should be sustained around activities and conversations. Later in the evening, energy might naturally decline as people become tired or ready to transition toward departure.

When energy levels don't match expectations, subtle adjustments can help realign the atmosphere. If energy is too low for the intended activity level, introducing a more engaging activity, changing music tempo, or simply moving people to different spaces can help. If energy is too high for intimate conversation, dimming lights, switching to quieter music, or creating more structured seating arrangements can encourage calmer interaction.

Individual comfort assessment means noticing when specific guests might need attention or support. This could be someone standing alone who needs introduction to ongoing conversation, someone who looks overwhelmed by group energy and might appreciate quieter interaction, or someone who seems ready to leave but doesn't know how to gracefully exit.

The key is developing intervention strategies that feel natural rather than obvious. Instead of announcing "Sarah looks lonely, let's all include her," you might approach Sarah with a specific conversational bridge: "Sarah, you have to hear Marcus's story about the hiking disaster." This creates inclusion without drawing attention to the social rescue operation.

Group dynamic assessment involves monitoring how different personalities are interacting and whether the mix is working well for everyone. Sometimes natural conversation flow creates perfect chemistry. Other times, certain combinations dominate while others get left out, or personality conflicts create tension that affects the overall atmosphere.

When group dynamics need adjustment, subtle redistribution often works better than dramatic intervention. You might suggest moving to different spaces for different activities, introduce new conversation topics that engage different people, or create opportunities for group composition to shift naturally through activities or transitions.

## Handling Conflicts and Difficult Guests with Quiet Confidence

Every host eventually encounters challenging social situations that require intervention: guests who drink too much, personality conflicts that create tension, or people whose behavior makes others uncomfortable. For introvert hosts, managing these situations requires strategies that work within your natural communication style rather than forcing confrontational approaches that drain your energy.

The approach I've landed on is what I'd call quiet authority: address the issue directly, without drama, without making it a moment. State the expectation once. Let the natural consequence do the work. The more emotional you get, the more energy it costs you and the worse the outcome.

For guests who are drinking too much, early intervention works better than waiting until problems escalate. This might mean switching to food service, introducing non-alcoholic beverage options, or simply being less available with drink refills. If direct conversation becomes necessary, private discussion works better than public correction: "I think you might want to slow down a bit, can I get you some water and food?"

Personality conflicts require careful navigation because your goal is maintaining overall party atmosphere rather than resolving underlying interpersonal issues. Sometimes separation strategies work well: engaging conflicting parties in different conversations or activities. Other times, topic redirection can defuse tension before it escalates.

When direct intervention becomes necessary, framing conflicts in terms of group comfort rather than personal judgment works more effectively: "Let's keep tonight's conversation light and fun" rather than "You're being inappropriate." This approach addresses behavior without attacking character, which often reduces defensiveness.

Different types of difficult behavior require different response strategies. The conversation dominator might respond well to structured activities that naturally distribute talking time. The person creating awkward tension might benefit from private check-in conversation to understand what's happening. The guest who's simply incompatible with the group might need gentle encouragement toward earlier departure.

Quiet confidence often resolves situations more effectively than dramatic intervention. When you address issues calmly and directly, most reasonable people respond positively. When you maintain clear boundaries without emotional escalation, you preserve both individual dignity and group comfort.

### When to Step In and When to Let Things Flow

Learning to distinguish between situations that require host intervention and situations that should be allowed to develop naturally is one of the most important skills for sustainable hosting. Over-management exhausts you and prevents guests from creating their own social experiences. Under-management allows problems to develop that could have been easily prevented.

The decision is simpler than it sounds: is someone uncomfortable, is something broken, or is everything fine? If someone is uncomfortable, step in. If something is broken, fix it. If everything is fine, leave it alone. Most of the time everything is fine and the hardest part is trusting that.

High-priority intervention situations include safety concerns, guests who are genuinely distressed or uncomfortable, behavior that's making multiple people uncomfortable, or practical issues that prevent normal party function. These situations require immediate host attention regardless of your energy level or other party priorities.

Medium-priority situations include minor social friction, uneven conversation participation, or logistical issues that could become problems if left unaddressed. These might warrant intervention if you have energy available and can address them subtly, but they don't require immediate action.

Low-priority situations include natural conversation lulls, minor personality differences, or temporary energy dips that are likely to resolve themselves. These situations often improve without intervention and may be disrupted by unnecessary host management.

Different personality types among your guests require different intervention thresholds. Introverted guests might need more support with inclusion and conversation entry points. Extroverted guests might need less direct attention but benefit from opportunities to exercise their social energy. Socially anxious guests might need reassurance and easy conversation opportunities.

The skill is recognizing when your intervention will improve situations versus when natural social processes are working effectively. When conversations are flowing, people are engaged, and group energy feels positive, stepping back and enjoying your own party often serves everyone better than constant hosting activity.

## Managing Your Own Energy Throughout the Event

Pushing through doesn't work. I've tried it, white-knuckling the last hour of a party when I'm already done, smiling at people while internally counting down. The guests can feel it even when they can't name it. What actually works is catching yourself before you hit the wall.

I check in with my actual energy level every 30-45 minutes and make adjustments based on what I find. Not anxious self-analysis: practical awareness that helps me host effectively for the whole event.

When energy levels are high, I can engage in more demanding hosting activities: supporting introductions, managing complex conversations, handling logistics that require decision-making. When energy levels are moderate, I focus on maintenance activities: keeping supplies stocked, monitoring overall atmosphere, being available for guest needs.

When energy levels are low, I shift to conservation mode: stepping back from active facilitation, engaging in less demanding conversation, focusing on practical tasks that provide legitimate reasons for reduced social engagement. This might mean spending time in the kitchen, checking on supplies, or having quieter one-on-one conversations rather than managing group dynamics.

Pacing yourself this way means you can be genuinely present for the whole evening rather than just surviving until people leave.

The voice that says a good host wouldn't need breaks has never actually hosted anything. It's describing a fictional person with unlimited social energy and no nervous system. You are a real person. Real people take breaks.

Different types of parties require different energy management strategies based on their duration, intensity, and social demands. Dinner parties typically have predictable energy curves that allow for planning around higher and lower demand periods. Casual gatherings might allow for more flexible energy management with natural breaks and transitions.

All-day events require sustained energy management with planned recharge breaks and distribution of hosting duties among multiple people. Professional events might require maintaining consistent energy levels for networking and relationship building throughout the duration.

## Creating Natural Conversation Bridges

One of the most valuable introvert hosting skills is supporting conversation connections without being constantly involved in every discussion. This requires strategic introduction techniques and conversation seeding that creates ongoing engagement without requiring your sustained attention.

The technique that works best: lead with a specific connection point rather than a generic introduction, then step back. Instead of 'Marcus, meet Elena,' try 'Marcus, Elena just got back from that photography workshop in Iceland you were asking about.' This gives people immediate conversation material and shows attention to their interests.

Context sharing enhances natural conversation development by providing background that helps people connect more easily. Mentioning someone's recent achievement, interesting project, or upcoming adventure gives others natural questions to ask and shows genuine attention to people's lives.

The goal is creating enough conversational momentum that discussions continue independently rather than requiring constant host facilitation. When people have genuine reasons to engage with each other, your job shifts from entertainment director to supportive observer who can step in when needed rather than managing every interaction.

## What to Actually Say: Scripts for Real Party Moments

The gap between 'here's the strategy' and 'here's what you actually say to real humans' is where a lot of hosting advice quietly falls apart. Here are exact scripts for the moments that catch introverts most off guard.

When you need to disappear for ten minutes: Don't just vanish; vanishing creates a void people notice. Give your exit a name. Try: 'I need to get the next course started, *Name*, can you make sure everyone's got a drink?' or 'I'm going to grab some more ice, back in a few.' Both are true, both give someone else a small task, and both explain your absence without making it strange.

When a conversation is dying and you're in it: 'Actually, I wanted to make sure I said hello to *Name* before the evening gets away from me, do you two know each other?' This exits you gracefully, potentially creates a new connection, and doesn't leave anyone standing alone.

When you need to rescue yourself (or a guest) from a conversation that won't end: 'I hate to pull *Name* away, but I promised to introduce them to *Other Name*, I'll bring them back.' Nobody argues with this. Nobody can.

*When you want people to start thinking about leaving: Stop refilling glasses. Bring out coffee or tea. Say 'I've had such a wonderful time tonight' in a warm, conclusive tone. If someone still doesn't move: 'I don't want to keep you too late, I know you've got an early morning tomorrow.' You're giving them a graceful exit, not evicting them.*

When introducing two strangers: Never just say their names. Add one specific thing: 'Marcus, this is Elena, she just got back from that photography trip to Iceland you were asking about last month.' Now they have somewhere to go. You can step away. Everyone wins.

When you're overwhelmed and need a moment: 'I'm just going to check on things in the kitchen, please help yourself to anything.' Then go stand in your kitchen for five minutes. Breathe. Eat something. Come back. This is not abandoning your guests. This is maintenance.

When a side conversation dies and the whole room goes quiet: This is the moment that can make a host spiral, the silence that lands on everyone at once and feels like your fault. It isn't. The move is to name something, not fix something. Pick the most recent thread anyone was pulling on and toss it back: 'Actually, I want to hear more about that, Marcus, you were saying something about the job change?' You're not inventing conversation, you're just giving the last thing someone said a second life. If nothing comes to you, pivot to food: 'Okay, who needs more wine?' gives everyone somewhere to look and breaks the spell. Silence at a table lasts about four seconds before it starts feeling long. You have time.

When someone asks what you do and you go blank: This happens because 'what do you do' is a bad question that demands a good answer instantly, and your brain locks up trying to compress your whole working life into something interesting. The solution is to have one line ready in advance, not an elevator pitch, just a plain sentence: 'I do X' or 'I work in X, mostly on Y.' Say that. If they want more they'll ask. If the blank still happens anyway: 'Honestly I never know how to answer that quickly, short version is X.' Admitting the question is hard makes you instantly more likeable than whoever gave the rehearsed answer.

When two people start an argument that's getting real: The low-drama move is to redirect rather than intervene. Wait for a breath, then come in across them, not at them: 'I want to circle back to what someone said earlier about X', or just pick up any thread from earlier in the evening and name it directly to someone else at the table. You're not shutting anyone down, you're just changing the subject loudly enough that they either follow or notice they've been noticed. If it's escalating past the point where redirection works, the direct version is: 'Let's keep tonight easy, you two can sort this out properly later.' Said warmly, without apology. Most people are relieved someone said it.

When you asked someone a question and completely stopped listening to the answer: This one is mortifying because you can see it happening in real time and can't stop it. When you come back and realize you've missed the last thirty seconds, don't pretend, just be honest: 'Sorry, I lost the thread for a second, can you say that last part again?' People find this charming rather than rude, especially if you immediately demonstrate that you're actually listening now. The alternative is nodding along hoping it was a yes/no question, getting caught, and feeling worse. Just ask.

When you realize you've been talking to one person for too long and everyone else has gone quiet: The graceful exit is to bring the room back in rather than just stopping. Finish your thought, then turn it outward: 'I'm monopolizing you, does anyone else have a take on this?' or 'I feel like I've been talking for an hour, I want to hear what you've all been discussing.' This acknowledges what happened without making it a big deal. The room comes back and you've done it in a way that models exactly the kind of generous hosting you're trying to do.

# Troubleshooting for the Overprepared Mind

Something will go wrong. I say this not to alarm you but to free you. The ice will run out. Someone will arrive an hour early. Two guests will discover they share a deeply inconvenient history. The playlist will inexplicably pivot to sad acoustic covers at full volume. This chapter is your contingency plan for the moment your carefully laid plan meets actual reality.

The party that taught me the most about crisis management wasn't one where everything went wrong; it was one where I thought everything had gone wrong, but my guests had a fantastic time anyway. I was hosting a birthday dinner for eight people when my carefully planned salmon turned out overcooked, my backup dessert collapsed in the oven, and my friend Jake showed up with his visiting cousin who I'd never met.

I spent the first hour of the party convinced I was a hosting failure, apologizing for food disasters while frantically trying to salvage the evening. But when I finally stopped catastrophizing and looked around, my guests were laughing about the cooking mishaps, Jake's cousin was fitting in perfectly with the group, and everyone was having genuine conversations over what I considered ruined food.

## Managing Unexpected Guests and No-Shows Gracefully

The surprise plus-one is every introvert host's nightmare scenario. You've planned for exactly eight people, bought food for exactly eight people, and arranged seating for exactly eight people. Then someone shows up with their visiting sister, their new boyfriend, or their friend who "was in the area and thought they'd say hi." Your carefully calibrated gathering suddenly feels overcrowded and under-resourced.

The key to handling unexpected guests is having buffer systems built into your planning rather than trying to improvise solutions in the moment. I always plan food for 10-15% more people than I've invited, keep emergency seating options available, and keep buffer capacity built into my party setup.

Food buffers work because most dishes can stretch further than you initially calculate. Pasta salads, soups, and casseroles naturally accommodate extra portions. Keep simple expansion foods available: good bread, cheese, fruit, or basic snacks that can become additional courses if needed. The goal isn't feeding unexpected guests gourmet meals, but ensuring everyone feels welcome and fed.

Seating flexibility prevents the awkward "musical chairs" situation where someone ends up sitting on a kitchen stool while everyone else has proper dinner seats. I keep folding chairs easily accessible and plan table arrangements that can accommodate one or two additional place settings without completely restructuring the space.

The psychological adjustment is often harder than the practical adjustment. When someone brings an unexpected guest, your first instinct might be panic about having enough food, adequate seating, or appropriate group dynamics. Take a breath before responding. Most surprise guests are understanding about informal accommodations, and most planned guests are flexible about slight adjustments to make newcomers feel welcome.

For no-shows, the opposite problem requires different emotional management. When several people cancel last-minute, your carefully planned eight-person dinner becomes a four-person gathering, which can feel like failure even though smaller groups often lead to better conversations.

I've learned to reframe no-shows as opportunities rather than disappointments. Smaller groups allow for deeper conversations, more intimate atmosphere, and often more relaxed hosting since you're managing fewer interpersonal dynamics. The food situation becomes abundance rather than scarcity, everyone gets generous portions and you have excellent leftovers.

The key is adjusting your hosting energy to match the actual group size rather than trying to maintain energy levels planned for larger gatherings. Smaller groups might benefit from more intimate conversation setups, different activity choices, or simply more relaxed pacing throughout the evening.

## Handling Social Disasters Without Internal Meltdown

Social disasters feel catastrophic when you're hosting because you feel personally responsible for everyone's experience. Someone spills wine on your furniture, two guests get into an argument about politics, or an awkward silence stretches on longer than feels comfortable. Your introvert brain immediately starts catastrophizing: the party is ruined, everyone is having a terrible time, you're a failure as a host.

Almost none of it matters as much as it feels like it does in the moment. I've hosted parties where I was convinced the whole thing was falling apart, and people left saying it was one of the best evenings they'd had. The thing that's going wrong is almost never the thing guests are experiencing.

I've developed a quick perspective check for when hosting panic starts to take over. I ask myself: Is anyone in danger? Is anyone genuinely distressed? Will this matter tomorrow? Usually the answers are no, no, and no, which helps me respond proportionally rather than catastrophically.

Spill management is one of the most common hosting anxieties, but it's also one of the easiest to handle well. Keep cleaning supplies easily accessible so you can respond quickly without creating drama. Most importantly, model the response you want from your guests; if you treat spills as minor inconveniences rather than major disasters, everyone else will too.

I've learned that the host's response to problems sets the tone for how guests experience them. When I laugh about cooking mishaps, guests feel free to find them amusing rather than concerning. When I handle spills calmly, guests don't feel guilty about accidents. When I treat unexpected changes as interesting developments rather than crises, the evening maintains positive energy.

Conversation disasters require more nuanced management but similar perspective. When someone brings up controversial topics that create tension, gentle redirection usually works better than confrontation: "Let's keep tonight light and fun, Sarah, tell us about your new job." When someone dominates conversation inappropriately, creating opportunities for others to contribute often balances participation naturally.

Your emotional response to problems affects your guests more than the actual problems do. When you maintain perspective and handle issues calmly, problems become minor blips rather than evening-defining disasters.

## Weather Emergencies and Backup Plans That Work

Moving an outdoor dinner party inside when it rained taught me the most important thing about weather backup plans: the backup needs to feel like a choice, not a consolation. If you move everything inside and treat it like a defeat, guests feel the disappointment. If you move everything inside and call it cozier, they go with it.

Indoor backup plans for outdoor events need to be complete alternatives, not just moving the same activities inside. What works in a backyard with open space might not work in a living room with furniture. Food that's perfect for outdoor grilling might need completely different preparation for indoor cooking. Activities that depend on outdoor space might need total replacement rather than just location changes.

I've learned to plan indoor alternatives that feel like deliberate choices rather than compromise solutions. Instead of "moving the barbecue inside," plan "cozy indoor gathering with comfort food." Instead of "cramming everyone into the living room," create "intimate conversation spaces with different seating areas." The reframing helps both you and your guests feel positive about necessary changes.

Guest communication during weather emergencies requires balance between keeping people informed and not creating panic about minor adjustments. Send updates early enough for people to adjust their expectations and arrival timing, but don't over-communicate about problems that might resolve themselves.

For different types of weather challenges, specific backup strategies work better than generic alternatives. Rain backup plans need to address wet arrivals, muddy shoes, coat storage, and potentially different arrival timing if driving conditions are affected. Heat backup plans need cooling strategies, shade alternatives, and possibly different food and drink choices that work better in high temperatures.

Cold weather backup plans might require different clothing considerations, heating adjustments, and food that provides warmth and comfort rather than light refreshment. Wind backup plans for outdoor events need to secure decorations, protect food service, and possibly modify activities that don't work in windy conditions.

I maintain weather contingency supplies year-round: umbrellas for unexpected rain, fans for heat waves, extra blankets for cold snaps, and secure storage for outdoor items that might need quick protection. These supplies live in easily accessible locations so I can implement weather plans quickly without adding stress to already challenging situations.

The psychological aspect of weather emergencies often creates more stress than the practical challenges. When you've planned an outdoor party and face indoor alternatives, it's natural to feel disappointed about changes to your vision. Allow yourself a few minutes to adjust emotionally, then focus on creating the best possible experience within the new parameters.

# Recovering from Hosting Mistakes Without Weeks of Regret

Introvert hosts are particularly vulnerable to post-party regret spirals because we tend to analyze social interactions intensely and assume that any awkward moments or imperfect elements reflect poorly on our hosting abilities. We replay conversations, obsess over food that didn't turn out perfectly, and convince ourselves that guests had terrible times because of our mistakes.

This post-party rumination is often more painful than any actual problems that occurred during the gathering. Most guests don't notice or remember the hosting imperfections that keep us awake replaying the evening. They remember whether they felt welcome, whether they had good conversations, and whether they enjoyed spending time with the people who were there.

I've developed a reality-check habit for when post-party regret starts taking over. I make myself list specific evidence that guests had a good time: did people stay longer than the minimum polite amount of time? Did anyone ask about future gatherings? Did conversations seem genuine and engaged? Did people seem relaxed and comfortable?

Usually the evidence contradicts my anxiety about hosting failures. People stayed late because they were enjoying themselves, not because they felt obligated. Conversations were animated because people were genuinely interested, not because they were politely filling silence. Guests complimented specific elements because they meant it, not because they were just being nice.

The perspective shift that helped me most was realizing that perfect hosting is not only impossible but also undesirable. Guests don't want to attend flawless performances; they want to spend time with people they care about in environments where they can be themselves. Minor imperfections often make gatherings more memorable and relatable than polished perfection.

The voice that's still replaying that one awkward pause from three Saturdays ago: it's lying about how bad it was. Nobody else remembers it. You're the only one who went home and wrote it a recurring role in your anxiety.

When actual mistakes do need addressing, simple acknowledgment usually works better than elaborate apologies or post-party damage control. If you burned the main dish, a brief "sorry dinner was a bit crispy" is sufficient; don't spend the next week texting everyone about your cooking failures. If conversation got awkward around a sensitive topic, moving forward is usually better than rehashing the moment.

### Learning When to Adapt and When to Persist

The best example I have of this: I once had an outdoor dinner party where it started raining an hour in. My first instinct was to apologize and scramble. What I actually did was move everyone inside, reframe it as cozier, and the night ended up being better than the version I'd planned. The skill isn't knowing what to do, it's not panicking long enough to find out what actually happens.

Adaptation works well when circumstances have genuinely changed in ways that affect guest comfort or safety. Moving an outdoor party inside due to severe weather, adjusting food service timing when several guests are delayed, or modifying activities when unexpected group dynamics require different approaches all represent appropriate adaptations.

Persistence works well when your original plan is sound but minor complications are creating temporary obstacles. Continuing with planned menu despite small cooking setbacks, maintaining planned timing despite one guest running late, or proceeding with intended activities despite initial resistance often leads to better outcomes than hasty changes.

The decision criteria involve assessing whether changes would genuinely improve the guest experience versus just reducing your hosting anxiety. Sometimes sticking with plans despite imperfections creates better results than switching to inferior backup options just to avoid potential problems.

Different personality types among your guests might influence adaptation decisions. Groups that appreciate spontaneity might enjoy flexible responses to changing circumstances. Groups that prefer structure might be more comfortable with hosts who maintain planned frameworks despite minor complications.

Hosting resilience comes from developing judgment and confidence rather than trying to prevent all possible problems. When you trust your ability to make good decisions in the moment, both adaptation and persistence become viable strategies depending on specific circumstances.

# Post-Party Cleanup and Recovery

The guests are gone. You did it. You are now standing in your home surrounded by empty glasses, abandoned napkins, and the particular silence that follows a room full of people. This chapter covers cleanup, yes, but mostly it covers you, and how to actually recover from the thing you just pulled off so you're not dreading the next one before it's even on the calendar.

The most deflating moment in hosting isn't when something goes wrong during the party; it's standing in your destroyed kitchen at midnight, looking at the mountain of dishes, wine-stained tablecloth, and mysterious sticky spots on your floor while your social battery is completely drained and you still have to function like a human being tomorrow.

I learned this the hard way after hosting what I thought was a perfect dinner party. The evening had been wonderful, great conversations, delicious food, guests who lingered because they were genuinely enjoying themselves. But when the last person left at 11 PM, I was faced with three hours of cleanup while running on pure social exhaustion. I ended up crying over a lasagna pan at 2 AM, not because the party was bad, but because I hadn't planned for the emotional and physical crash that comes after successful hosting.

That experience taught me that cleanup isn't just about returning your space to normal; it's about managing the transition from social hosting mode back to private recovery mode while handling practical tasks that can't wait until tomorrow. Good cleanup systems preserve your energy for recovery while ensuring your space and relationships don't suffer from post-party neglect.

## Recruiting Guest Help for Cleanup (The Right Way)

One of the most effective but underused strategies for manageable post-party cleanup is enlisting willing guests to help with basic restoration tasks. Many people enjoy helping clean up because it provides a way to show appreciation for hosting while extending social time in a more intimate, collaborative setting.

You can usually tell who means it. The person who actually wants to help has already started stacking plates before you've said anything. They're looking for something to carry. Give them a job. The person offering out of politeness is already eyeing their coat; let them go.

I've learned to accept help gracefully instead of insisting that guests shouldn't have to clean. A simple "that would be amazing, thank you" works much better than "oh no, you don't need to do that" followed by awkward negotiation. When people offer help, they usually mean it, and declining can make them feel less useful.

Task delegation for guest helpers works best when you provide specific, bounded tasks instead of general "help with whatever" instructions. "Could you load the dishwasher while I put away leftovers?" or "Would you mind wiping down the table while I handle the kitchen?" gives people clear objectives that don't require decision-making about your personal systems.

The timing of guest cleanup help typically works best with the last 2-3 people remaining instead of trying to organize group cleanup while most guests are still focused on socializing. As the party naturally winds down, willing helpers often become apparent through their lingering and offers of assistance.

Different types of guests bring different cleanup strengths. Your organized friend might excel at systematic dishwashing or leftover organization. Your practical friend might be great at furniture restoration or basic cleaning tasks. Your naturally helpful friend might enjoy coordinating multiple cleanup tasks while you focus on food storage.

Family-style cleanup can become a pleasant wind-down activity when managed well. People who enjoyed the gathering often appreciate extending their time through collaborative restoration while having more intimate conversations that wouldn't have been possible during the larger group setting.

The boundary-setting aspect is crucial: make it clear that help is appreciated but not expected, and provide easy exit opportunities for people who prefer to leave. "Thank you so much for offering, if you need to head out, that's totally fine, but if you want to stay and chat while we tidy up, I'd love the company."

Some of the better conversations I've had at my own parties happened over the dishes afterward, when it was down to two or three people and nobody had anywhere to be.

## Immediate Post-Party Cleanup: The Essential Minimums

The key to manageable post-party cleanup is identifying what absolutely must be done immediately versus what can wait until you have more energy. When you're socially and physically depleted, decision-making becomes difficult, so having predetermined priorities prevents you from either doing too much (exhausting yourself further) or too little (creating problems for tomorrow).

The goal is crisis-prevention cleanup only: handling tasks that would create genuine problems if left until the next day. Food safety issues, spill damage prevention, securing valuable items, basic sanitation that affects your ability to function normally tomorrow. That's it.

Food safety tasks take priority because they can't be delayed without health risks. This means refrigerating perishable leftovers, disposing of food that's been sitting at room temperature too long, and getting dairy products and meat dishes properly stored. These tasks require immediate attention regardless of how tired you are.

Spill damage prevention involves addressing liquid spills that could stain furniture or flooring if left overnight. Red wine, coffee, or grease spots need immediate attention, but this doesn't mean deep cleaning; just basic damage control to prevent permanent staining. Keep simple cleaning supplies easily accessible for quick spill response.

Securing valuables and clearing walkways prevents loss or damage from leaving expensive items scattered around tired hosts' spaces. This includes expensive serving pieces, electronic equipment, or borrowed items that need protection. Also ensure walkways are clear of obstacles that could cause falls when you're tired and moving around in low light.

Basic sanitation covers tasks that would interfere with normal life functions if left undone. This might mean clearing enough dishes to have breakfast plates available, ensuring bathroom supplies are restocked, or handling obvious hygiene issues without attempting complete deep cleaning.

For different types of gatherings, immediate cleanup priorities shift based on the activities and spaces involved. Outdoor parties might require securing decorations against weather, bringing expensive items inside, or handling food that's been in temperature danger zones. Gaming events might emphasize protecting expensive equipment and organizing games that could be damaged if left scattered.

Professional gatherings at your home might require extra attention to restoring appropriate work-life boundaries, ensuring confidential materials are secured, and returning your space to personal rather than business use quickly.

I always include "host recovery prep" in immediate cleanup: setting out comfortable clothes, ensuring you have easy breakfast options available, and preparing your bedroom for immediate rest when cleanup is finished. These small preparations make the transition to recovery much smoother.

Immediate cleanup should take no more than 30-45 minutes and should focus on preventing problems rather than achieving cleanliness. Everything else can wait until you have more energy and better decision-making capacity.

# Strategic Next-Day Cleanup Systems

The day after a party I'm usually good for about one real task. If I try to do a full kitchen restoration and laundry and putting the living room back together, I end up doing all of them badly. The better move is picking the one thing that will bother me most if it's not done, doing that, and leaving the rest for when I have actual energy.

I've developed a recovery-friendly cleanup approach that breaks tasks into manageable chunks based on energy requirements and timing flexibility. High-energy tasks that require decision-making or physical effort get scheduled for when you naturally have the most capacity. Low-energy tasks that can be done while resting get saved for energy dips.

Morning cleanup typically works best for dishwashing and kitchen restoration because these tasks benefit from natural energy and can provide satisfying accomplishment early in the day. However, if you're genuinely exhausted, pushing through morning cleanup often backfires and makes the entire day more difficult.

I assess my actual energy level on party recovery days rather than forcing predetermined cleanup schedules. If I wake up feeling surprisingly good, I might tackle major cleanup projects early. If I'm completely drained, I might limit morning activities to essential tasks and save major cleanup for later in the day or even the weekend.

Afternoon cleanup often works well for organizing and putting away items because these tasks require less physical energy but benefit from better decision-making capacity than you might have immediately after the party. This is when I sort through leftover food, return borrowed items to proper storage, and handle mail or personal tasks that accumulated during party preparation.

Evening cleanup can include gentle, restorative tasks like folding table linens, organizing photos from the party, or writing thank-you messages. These activities provide closure on the hosting experience while being manageable when you're tired but not ready for sleep.

Different recovery patterns require different cleanup timing strategies. Some people bounce back quickly and prefer getting cleanup completely finished the day after hosting. Others need several days to fully recover and benefit from spreading cleanup tasks across multiple days.

For people with demanding work schedules, weekend hosting might require cleanup strategies that work around Monday work obligations. For people with family responsibilities, cleanup planning needs to account for childcare and household management duties that can't be postponed.

## Leftover Management and Food Storage

Leftover food management is one of the most overlooked aspects of post-party cleanup, but it significantly affects both your immediate recovery and your food budget for the following week. Good leftover strategies can provide easy meals during your recovery period while preventing food waste and storage problems.

I plan leftover management during menu planning rather than trying to figure out food storage when I'm tired after hosting. This includes having appropriate storage containers available, understanding which dishes freeze well, and knowing which items should be consumed quickly versus stored for later use.

Immediate food safety requires getting perishable items properly refrigerated within safe time limits, regardless of how tired you are. This isn't negotiable; food safety issues can't be delayed without health risks. However, you can simplify this process by having storage containers easily accessible and pre-planning which items need immediate attention.

Creative leftover transformation can turn party food into easy meals for your recovery period. Roasted vegetables become soup ingredients. Cheese and bread become easy lunches. Desserts provide comfort food for post-party emotional recovery. Planning these transformations in advance makes leftover management feel like meal planning assistance rather than cleanup burden.

Leftover sharing with guests can reduce your storage burden while providing thoughtful gestures that strengthen hosting relationships. Sending guests home with care packages of party food often generates more appreciation than the original meal and solves storage problems simultaneously.

Different types of party food have different leftover management requirements. Buffet-style parties might generate large quantities of mixed leftovers that need creative organization. Plated dinner parties might produce smaller quantities of specific items that store more easily. Potluck gatherings might result in diverse leftovers that require different storage approaches.

For dietary restriction considerations, leftover management becomes more complex when you need to maintain separation between different dietary categories. Gluten-free items need separate storage from regular items. Vegetarian and meat dishes require different handling procedures. These considerations affect both immediate storage and longer-term leftover planning.

Holiday parties often generate larger quantities of special occasion foods that might not store well or might require different preservation methods than everyday meals. Understanding how to handle traditional holiday foods prevents waste while maximizing the value of expensive seasonal ingredients.

## Deep Cleaning vs. Maintenance Cleaning Decisions

One of the most important post-party decisions is determining what level of cleaning is necessary versus what level feels psychologically necessary when you're tired and overwhelmed.

Over-cleaning wastes energy you need for recovery, while under-cleaning can create ongoing stress that interferes with your return to normal life.

I use a "functionality test" to determine cleaning priorities: what level of cleanliness is needed for normal life function versus aesthetic preference? Sticky floors need immediate attention because they interfere with basic movement. Slightly messy tabletops can wait because they don't affect daily function.

The "host guilt" factor often drives unnecessary deep cleaning when standard maintenance cleaning would be sufficient. The feeling that your space should be pristine because you hosted guests is understandable but often counterproductive when you're already depleted from the social and physical demands of entertaining.

Seasonal cleaning considerations affect post-party cleanup decisions because some times of year naturally require more thorough cleaning than others. Post-holiday party cleanup might coincide with annual deep cleaning projects. Summer party cleanup might require different approaches due to open windows and outdoor elements.

Professional versus personal gathering cleanup has different standards based on the relationships involved and potential future interactions. Business entertaining might require higher cleanliness standards because colleagues or clients might return to your space. Personal friend gatherings might allow for more relaxed cleanup approaches.

Different types of social gatherings create different cleaning requirements based on the activities involved. Gaming parties might require organization and equipment care more than deep cleaning. Dinner parties might emphasize kitchen restoration and dining area cleaning. Outdoor parties might focus on weather protection and equipment storage.

The energy cost-benefit analysis of immediate deep cleaning versus delayed thorough cleaning often favors delayed approaches when you're already exhausted. Light maintenance cleaning immediately, followed by more thorough cleaning when you have energy, typically produces better results than attempting complete deep cleaning when you're tired.

I maintain different cleaning standards for different life circumstances. During busy periods, basic functionality cleaning might be sufficient. During relaxed periods, more thorough cleaning might be enjoyable and restorative. Understanding your personal cleaning needs and energy patterns helps guide appropriate post-party cleaning decisions.

## Recovery Planning and Personal Care

Post-party recovery involves much more than just cleaning; it includes emotional recovery from social interaction, physical recovery from hosting demands, and practical recovery of your normal life routines. Planning for this recovery is as important as planning the party itself, especially for introverts who need substantial downtime after social events.

Recovery day is real. I used to push through, do the full cleanup, answer all the texts, be a functional person. Now I plan for the day after the same way I plan for the party itself. Low commitments. Easy food. Permission to do nothing useful. The post-party crash isn't weakness. It's the bill coming due for the energy you spent. Pay it without guilt and you'll host again sooner.

I treat the day after hosting as a recovery day with modified expectations for productivity and social interaction. This might mean declining social invitations, postponing demanding tasks, or planning gentler activities that support rather than deplete recovery energy.

Physical recovery considerations include managing the fatigue that comes from extended social interaction, physical activity during party preparation and hosting, and often irregular sleep schedules around party timing. This might require extra sleep, gentle movement, or comfort activities that restore physical energy.

Emotional recovery from hosting involves processing the social interactions, evaluating the success of the gathering, and managing any hosting anxiety or perfectionism that might interfere with satisfaction with the event. This processing time is crucial for building hosting confidence and enjoyment.

Social recovery means managing your social energy carefully in the days following hosting to prevent social burnout that could affect your willingness to host future gatherings. This might mean declining additional social commitments or limiting social media engagement that extends social energy demands.

Different personality types within your household might have different recovery needs that affect post-party planning. Extroverted partners might want to process the party through discussion, while introverted hosts might need quiet reflection time. Children might need extra attention if family routines were disrupted by hosting preparation.

Work schedule considerations affect recovery planning because hosting often occurs on weekends before work weeks that don't accommodate extended recovery time. Planning hosting schedules and recovery needs around work obligations prevents hosting from negatively affecting professional performance.

The goal of recovery planning isn't extended hibernation but rather appropriate restoration that allows you to return to normal life with positive memories of hosting rather than exhaustion and stress that discourages future entertaining.

# Special Occasions and Themed Events

Themed parties are where introvert planning instincts and extrovert-scale ambitions collide most spectacularly. The good news: introverts are genuinely excellent at themed events because we actually care about the details that make a theme feel immersive rather than half-hearted. The slightly complicated news: themed parties invite scope creep, and scope creep is the enemy of actually enjoying the thing you spent three weeks obsessing over.

The most memorable party I ever threw wasn't the most elaborate or expensive; it was my friend Marcus's 30th birthday, where we transformed my living room into a makeshift Star Trek bridge. Half the guests came in Starfleet uniforms, we served "replicator food" (really good takeout), and we spent the evening discussing fictional starship protocols with the same seriousness other people reserve for actual important topics.

What made that party special wasn't the theme itself, but how the theme gave everyone permission to be enthusiastically nerdy together. People who might normally make polite small talk were debating Federation policy and comparing uniform accuracy. The structure of the theme created instant conversation material and shared experience, while the playful nature of the whole thing eliminated social pressure to be sophisticated or impressive.

## Understanding Your Audience: Matching Themes to Communities

The Star Trek party I threw for Marcus worked because Marcus and his friends have strong opinions about Federation policy. The same party would have been a disaster with my book club. Theme choice isn't about what looks impressive; it's about whether your specific guests will be able to run with it.

I've learned to think about themes as conversation and connection facilitators rather than decorative choices. The best themes provide natural talking points, shared references, and opportunities for people to express interests they're genuinely passionate about. When themes align with your guests' existing enthusiasms, the party practically runs itself.

Successful themes feel like natural extensions of your guests' existing interests rather than costumes they have to put on for your party. When themes align with genuine enthusiasms, people arrive excited to participate rather than wondering how to fake interest in something unfamiliar.

The worst themed party I ever attended had an elaborate concept, expensive decorations, and a host who spent the whole night making sure everyone appreciated the theme. Nobody was allowed to just have a good time; we were supposed to be having a Themed Time. The best themed parties I've hosted barely felt like themed parties from the inside. They felt like gatherings where everyone happened to care about the same thing.

## Renaissance Faire and Historical Themes: Creating Immersive Experiences

Historical and Renaissance themed parties work well when the theme does the heavy lifting. People who love this world arrive already in character, already with opinions, already looking for someone to debate with. Your job is almost entirely setup: the right atmosphere, enough food, enough space. Then get out of the way.

The people I've hosted from the Renaissance faire world don't need me to do anything elaborate. They bring their own energy and their own opinions. My job is to create a space that doesn't fight what they've got going on: candles instead of overhead lights, rich fabrics, room for the capes.

Costume considerations require careful balance between encouraging participation and avoiding pressure on people who aren't comfortable with elaborate dress-up. Make costumes clearly optional and provide simple alternatives for people who want to participate without major costume investment. A simple cloak or medieval-inspired shirt can help someone feel included without requiring extensive preparation.

Food presentation can support historical themes without requiring authentic period recipes. Serving familiar foods in period-appropriate ways (bread bowls, shared platters, simple presentations) creates atmosphere while ensuring everyone finds something they want to eat. Focus on abundance and sharing rather than historical accuracy.

Activities that support historical themes include storytelling, simple period games, music appreciation, or craft demonstrations. The goal is providing structure for interaction within the theme rather than elaborate entertainment programs that require specialized knowledge or skills.

## Holiday Celebrations That Don't Overwhelm

Holiday parties present unique challenges for introvert hosts because they often come with predetermined expectations, family obligations, and seasonal stress that compounds normal hosting anxiety. The solution is creating holiday celebrations that honor the spirit of the season while maintaining your hosting sanity and guest comfort.

The key to successful holiday hosting is focusing on one or two meaningful elements rather than trying to recreate elaborate traditional celebrations. Choose aspects of holiday traditions that genuinely resonate with you and your guests, then build simple celebrations around those elements rather than feeling obligated to include every traditional component.

I hosted Christmas dinner for twelve people the year after my mother died. I had no interest in doing any of it and almost cancelled twice. What I ended up with was the simplest possible version: one good main dish, things people brought, candles, her favorite playlist. It was the best Christmas dinner I've hosted. Not because I worked hard at it. Because I stopped trying to replicate something and just made something real.

For winter holidays, focus on elements that create warmth and connection rather than elaborate presentations. Simple seasonal foods, warm drinks, cozy lighting, and opportunities for people to share holiday memories or traditions can create meaningful celebration without overwhelming preparation requirements.

Holiday music requires careful selection because people have strong personal associations with seasonal songs. Choose instrumental versions of familiar tunes, or focus on general winter/seasonal music rather than specifically religious or culturally specific selections unless you know your guest demographics well.

Gift exchange activities can enhance holiday gatherings when designed thoughtfully. Simple exchanges with modest spending limits, creative challenges like homemade gifts, or charitable giving activities can provide holiday spirit without creating financial pressure or gift anxiety for participants.

Spring and summer holiday celebrations often work well with outdoor elements and lighter, fresher approaches. Seasonal food celebrations, garden parties with spring themes, or simple outdoor gatherings that acknowledge longer days and warmer weather can capture holiday spirit without requiring elaborate indoor decorating.

Different cultural backgrounds among your guests require sensitive holiday planning that acknowledges diversity rather than assuming universal holiday traditions. Focus on secular seasonal elements, or explicitly acknowledge that you're celebrating specific traditions while welcoming people from different backgrounds.

The timing of holiday parties affects both your stress level and guest availability. Hosting holiday celebrations slightly before or after actual holidays often reduces scheduling conflicts and allows for more relaxed celebration without competing with family obligations or other social commitments.

## Sports Events and Game Day Gatherings

Sports-themed gatherings have completely different requirements from other party types because the event itself provides structure, timing, and entertainment. Your job as host shifts from creating engagement to supporting the viewing experience and managing practical logistics around sustained group attention to external entertainment.

Game day hosting requires understanding your guests' investment levels in the sport and teams involved. Serious fans need different accommodations than casual viewers who are mainly there for social experience. Plan food, seating, and noise levels accordingly based on whether you're hosting dedicated fans or social viewers.

Food for sports events needs to be substantial, easy to eat while standing or sitting casually, and available continuously rather than served at specific times. People will eat throughout the game based on excitement levels and natural breaks rather than formal meal timing. Plan for higher consumption during exciting moments and halftime periods.

Seating arrangements should prioritize sight lines to screens rather than conversation facilitation. People need to be able to see clearly without constantly adjusting positions. Consider sound levels too; serious fans might want volume high enough to hear commentary clearly, while social viewers might prefer quieter background levels that allow conversation.

For mixed groups that include both serious fans and casual attendees, create multiple engagement options. Set up the main viewing area for dedicated watching, with secondary spaces where people can socialize more casually while still following the game. This prevents conflicts between different viewing styles.

Team loyalty considerations can create social dynamics that require careful management. If your guests support opposing teams, light-hearted rivalry can enhance the experience, but serious conflicts might need intervention. Know your guests well enough to predict whether team differences will create fun competition or genuine tension.

## Role-Playing and Gaming Themed Events

Role-playing themed parties can range from casual gatherings where people discuss favorite games and characters to immersive events where guests create characters for party-specific scenarios. Match the complexity to your guests' experience levels and enthusiasm for active participation versus casual conversation about gaming interests.

For experienced gaming groups, collaborative storytelling activities, character creation workshops, or themed discussions about favorite gaming experiences can provide engaging party content. These activities work because they tap into existing skills and interests while creating opportunities for sharing gaming experiences and creative ideas.

Gaming-themed food and drink can support the atmosphere without requiring elaborate preparation. Tavern-style foods, themed cocktails with creative names, or simple presentations that reference popular games can enhance the experience. Focus on foods that won't damage gaming equipment if people want to play during the party.

Equipment considerations become important for gaming-themed events because participants might bring valuable games, books, or accessories. Provide secure storage areas and stable surfaces for gaming materials. Consider space requirements for different types of games if you're planning actual gaming activities during the party.

Mixed groups that include both experienced gamers and newcomers require careful activity planning that includes rather than excludes people with different experience levels. Choose activities that don't require extensive gaming knowledge, or provide introductory elements that help newcomers participate meaningfully.

The social dynamics of gaming communities often include shared references, inside jokes, and technical discussions that can be exclusive to outsiders. As host, support inclusion by providing context for gaming references and creating opportunities for experienced players to share their enthusiasm without alienating newcomers.

## Birthday Celebrations Across Different Age Groups and Communities

Birthday parties require balancing the guest of honor's preferences with the social dynamics of their friend groups and family members. Successful birthday hosting involves understanding what type of celebration would genuinely please the birthday person rather than implementing generic party formulas.

For adult birthday celebrations, the focus often shifts from entertainment-heavy children's party models to social connection opportunities that acknowledge the person's interests, relationships, and life stage. The celebration should reflect the birthday person's personality and social preferences rather than party planning conventions.

Milestone birthdays (30th, 40th, 50th, etc.) might warrant more elaborate celebration or special recognition, but they also require sensitivity to how the birthday person feels about aging and public attention. Some people want big celebrations for major birthdays, while others prefer low-key acknowledgment with close friends.

The birthday person's social energy and preference for attention should guide celebration planning more than external expectations about what birthday parties should include. Introverted birthday people might prefer intimate dinners with close friends. Extroverted birthday people might enjoy larger, more energetic celebrations.

Age-appropriate celebration elements become important when planning birthday parties that include multiple generations or diverse age groups. Activities, music, food, and timing should accommodate the age range of attendees while still focusing on the birthday person's preferences.

Gift-giving coordination can enhance birthday celebrations when handled thoughtfully. Group gifts for significant birthdays, charitable donations in the birthday person's name, or experience gifts that create ongoing memories can be more meaningful than individual presents while reducing gift-giving pressure on attendees.

## Creating Memorable Experiences Within Your Hosting Capacity

The most important insight about themed and special occasion hosting is that memorable experiences come from genuine connection and shared enthusiasm rather than elaborate production values or expensive elements. Your hosting energy is better spent supporting authentic interaction around shared interests than trying to create impressive displays.

Successful themed events work within your natural hosting strengths and energy capacity rather than requiring you to become an event production specialist. Choose themes that genuinely interest you and match your guests' enthusiasms. Focus on one or two meaningful elements rather than trying to create comprehensive themed experiences.

The Star Trek party for Marcus worked because I did almost nothing. I mentioned the theme, suggested people come in costume if they wanted, made a lot of food, and stepped back. What happened next required zero facilitation from me; people who had never met were arguing about the Dominion War for three hours. My job was to create the container. The guests filled it.

The goal is creating frameworks that support genuine connection and shared experience rather than staging performances for your guests to attend. When themes provide natural conversation material and opportunities for people to share their interests and enthusiasm, the party content develops organically without requiring constant host entertainment.

# Growing Your Hosting Confidence

Hosting confidence doesn't come from reading about hosting. It comes from hosting, surviving it, noticing what worked, and doing it again slightly less terrified than before. This chapter won't give you confidence, only experience can do that. But it will show you how to build it faster and more deliberately than just hoping it shows up on its own.

The transformation from anxious host to confident host doesn't happen overnight, and it definitely doesn't happen by throwing yourself into the deep end with elaborate parties for 20 people. I learned this the hard way when I decided that hosting one successful dinner party for six people meant I was ready to throw a housewarming for 25 guests. The result was an overwhelming evening where I spent most of the party hiding in my kitchen, stress-eating leftover appetizers while my guests politely mingled without me.

## Scaling Up Gradually Without Losing Your Sanity

The biggest mistake introvert hosts make when building confidence is jumping from small successes to dramatically larger challenges without developing the intermediate skills and systems needed to handle increased complexity. Going from intimate dinners to large parties isn't just a numbers game; it requires completely different hosting approaches, logistics management, and energy conservation strategies.

What works is adding one challenging element at a time while keeping everything else within your proven comfort zone. If you've successfully hosted six people, try eight people with the same menu and setup you know works. If you've mastered casual dinners, try one special occasion dinner with familiar guests. If you're comfortable with close friends, try adding one new person to a proven group dynamic.

Each new challenge should build on established strengths rather than requiring you to develop multiple new skills simultaneously. When you try to scale up guest count, complexity, and formality all at once, you create a perfect storm of stress that can set back your hosting confidence significantly.

I track my hosting capacity like athletes track their training progress. After each party, I note what felt manageable, what pushed my limits, and what exceeded my capacity. This data helps me plan appropriate next steps rather than guessing about what I can handle. If hosting eight people felt comfortable, maybe I can try ten. If a three-hour party left me energized, maybe I can experiment with four hours.

Different aspects of hosting can be scaled independently based on your specific strengths and challenges. Some introverts find it easier to increase guest count while keeping food simple. Others prefer complex menus with smaller groups. Some can handle longer parties with familiar people, while others do better with shorter gatherings that include new guests.

Logistical scaling often requires the biggest adjustments as parties grow larger. Your systems for food preparation, space management, and guest coordination need to evolve as numbers increase. What works for six people (cooking everything yourself, using your regular dishes, having one conversation area) might not work for twelve people without significant modification.

I've learned to test new logistical systems before implementing them at actual parties. If I want to try buffet-style service instead of plated dinners, I'll experiment with family or very close friends first. If I'm considering a new space arrangement, I'll test it during a casual gathering before using it for a special occasion.

Energy management becomes more complex as parties scale up, requiring more sophisticated strategies for maintaining hosting capacity throughout larger events. What works for small gatherings, brief kitchen breaks, quiet conversations during transitions, might not be sufficient for larger, longer parties that require sustained social energy.

The goal isn't reaching some arbitrary party size that proves you're a "real" host. The goal is finding your optimal hosting sweet spot where you can create meaningful experiences without depleting yourself. For some introverts, that might be intimate dinners for four people. For others, it might be casual gatherings for fifteen. Both are completely valid hosting achievements.

## Building a Support Network of Fellow Introverted Hosts

One of the most isolating aspects of developing hosting confidence is feeling like you're the only person who finds entertaining stressful and exhausting. Most hosting advice comes from people who seem naturally energized by large gatherings, leaving introvert hosts feeling like there's something wrong with their approach to social interaction.

Finding other introvert hosts who understand your challenges and can share practical strategies makes an enormous difference in building confidence and developing hosting practices that last. These relationships provide both emotional support and practical knowledge that you can't get from generic hosting advice or extroverted friends who don't understand your energy management needs.

I actively seek out other hosts who seem to approach entertaining thoughtfully rather than energetically. These are often people who throw smaller, more intimate gatherings, who plan carefully in advance, who create comfortable environments rather than high-energy entertainments. They might not identify as introverts, but their hosting style suggests they understand the value of sustainable, thoughtful entertaining.

Professional networks often include people with event planning experience who understand the behind-the-scenes work that goes into successful gatherings. These contacts can provide practical advice about vendor relationships, logistics management, and contingency planning that applies to personal hosting as well as professional events.

Online communities of introvert hosts provide valuable support and idea sharing without requiring face-to-face social energy. Social media groups, forums, and blogs focused on thoughtful entertaining often include people who share your hosting philosophy and can offer tested strategies for common challenges.

Local community groups around specific interests often include natural hosts who organize gatherings for fellow enthusiasts. Book clubs, hiking groups, craft circles, and hobby organizations frequently include people who have developed hosting skills while organizing group activities around shared interests.

The exchange of hosting duties with other confident hosts creates mutual support while reducing individual hosting burden. Instead of feeling obligated to host every gathering yourself, developing relationships with other hosts allows for shared responsibility and learning opportunities.

I've learned to be explicit about seeking hosting advice and support rather than assuming other people don't struggle with entertaining challenges. Many people who appear naturally confident about hosting have developed systems and strategies through experience, and they're often willing to share knowledge with others who are working to improve their skills.

Mentorship relationships with more experienced hosts can provide valuable guidance and encouragement, especially when you find hosts whose style aligns with your personality and values. These relationships don't need to be formal, simply expressing interest in learning from someone's hosting approach often leads to helpful conversations and advice.

## Learning When to Say No and When to Stretch Your Comfort Zone

I've gotten better at saying no to hosting situations that aren't right for where I am. Not every gathering I'm invited to host is one I should host. Some years I host a lot. Some years I don't, because other things are taking the energy. That's not failure, that's knowing yourself.

Before I say yes to any hosting obligation, I run a quick check: energy levels, current life stress, available prep time, emotional bandwidth. If multiple factors are already stretched, adding hosting usually leads to a bad experience that sets back rather than builds confidence.

Timing considerations affect hosting capacity significantly. Hosting during particularly busy work periods, family stress, or other life challenges often results in either canceling plans (disappointing guests) or pushing through with inadequate preparation (creating stressful experiences). Learning to recognize when timing isn't right prevents both scenarios.

The type of gathering matters as much as the timing when deciding whether to accept hosting challenges. Intimate dinners with close friends require different energy than professional networking events or celebrations for acquaintances. Understanding which types of social interaction energize you versus drain you helps guide decisions about hosting opportunities.

Guest list considerations influence whether specific hosting opportunities will support or undermine your confidence development. Hosting people who are understanding about imperfections and supportive of your efforts creates positive experiences that build confidence. Hosting critical or high-maintenance people before you feel ready can create setbacks that take time to recover from.

However, some discomfort is necessary for growth, and learning to distinguish between productive challenge and overwhelming stress requires experience and self-awareness. Productive challenges push you slightly beyond your current comfort zone while still being manageable with effort and preparation. Overwhelming challenges require skills or capacity you don't currently possess.

I've developed clear criteria to guide these decisions. Good growth opportunities involve one new challenge while keeping other elements familiar (new guest, familiar menu; larger group, familiar space; special occasion, trusted friends). Poor growth opportunities involve multiple new challenges simultaneously or challenges that don't build on existing strengths.

The social pressure to accept hosting responsibilities can be intense, especially around holidays, special occasions, or when you're the person in a group who "usually hosts." Learning to resist this pressure when accepting would compromise your hosting quality or personal wellbeing requires practice and confidence in your own judgment.

Alternative contribution strategies let you participate in group social activities without taking on full hosting responsibility. Offering to co-host, providing specific assistance (food, setup, cleanup), or hosting smaller preliminary gatherings can maintain social connections while managing your hosting capacity appropriately.

## Developing Your Signature Hosting Style

My hosting style is: good food that's mostly done before anyone arrives, a space arranged so people aren't all looking at each other waiting for something to happen, and a few people I actually want to talk to. That's it. I spent years thinking I was doing it wrong because it wasn't more elaborate. I wasn't.

I've learned that effective hosting styles emerge from understanding what you genuinely enjoy about bringing people together and building systems that support those elements while minimizing aspects that drain your energy. Some introverts love menu planning and cooking but find conversation facilitation exhausting. Others enjoy creating beautiful environments but prefer simple food that doesn't require last-minute preparation.

My own signature style has evolved around conversation-focused hosting: comfortable environments where people can talk, while I stay out of the way unless needed. This means excellent food that doesn't require active cooking during the party, beautiful but not elaborate table settings, and activities that support deep conversation rather than high-energy entertainment.

The development process involves experimenting with different approaches while paying attention to which elements feel energizing versus draining. Do you enjoy elaborate food preparation or prefer simple, high-quality ingredients? Do you like creating themed environments or prefer understated elegance? Do you enjoy supporting group activities or prefer creating space for organic interaction?

I maintain a "hosting values" list that guides decisions about party planning and helps ensure my hosting style remains authentic rather than driven by external expectations or social pressure. These values include prioritizing genuine connection over impressive presentation, creating inclusive environments where different personality types feel comfortable, and maintaining lasting practices that let me enjoy my own gatherings.

Signature hosting styles often include specific elements that become associated with your gatherings: your excellent coffee, your comfortable seating arrangements, your thoughtful question prompts, your beautiful music selection. These signature elements create consistency that guests appreciate while reflecting your personal interests and strengths.

The goal isn't developing a hosting style that impresses everyone or works for every possible social situation. The goal is creating an approach that feels authentic to you, works within your energy capacity, and reliably creates positive experiences for the specific people you most enjoy hosting.

Documentation of successful hosting elements helps refine and maintain your signature style over time. I keep notes about menu combinations that work well, space arrangements that support good conversation, timing patterns that feel comfortable, and guest combinations that create positive chemistry. This information helps me replicate successes while continuing to refine my approach.

## Overcoming Hosting Setbacks and Building Resilience

Every host, regardless of experience level, encounters parties that don't go as planned, guests who create challenges, or situations that test their confidence and problem-solving abilities. Building hosting resilience means developing the ability to learn from difficult experiences rather than being discouraged by them.

I've learned to distinguish between hosting failures that reflect inadequate preparation or poor judgment and hosting challenges that arise from uncontrollable factors or unreasonable guest behavior. Taking responsibility for genuine mistakes while not personalizing problems caused by external factors helps maintain realistic confidence levels.

Post-party analysis helps identify specific lessons from challenging experiences without falling into general self-criticism about hosting abilities. What specific elements didn't work well? What could be planned differently next time? What aspects were successful despite overall difficulties? This targeted analysis produces practical insights rather than vague anxiety about future hosting.

Recovery strategies for hosting confidence include returning to proven successful approaches before attempting new challenges, seeking support from understanding friends or fellow hosts, and deliberately planning low-stakes gatherings that rebuild positive hosting experiences. Sometimes confidence recovery requires stepping back to smaller, simpler gatherings temporarily.

The perspective that helps most with hosting setbacks is remembering that guests' experiences are often much more positive than hosts realize. What feels like failure to someone managing all the logistics often feels like an enjoyable, authentic gathering to people who are focused on social connection rather than operational details.

The voice that says 'I'm just not a party person' is confusing a personality trait with a skill set. Introverts aren't bad at hosting. They're bad at hosting like extroverts. That's a different problem, and one that's entirely solvable.

Resilience also means developing comfort with imperfection and learning to model relaxed responses to problems for your guests. When hosts handle minor disasters with humor and grace, guests often remember those moments as highlights rather than problems. Your response to challenges affects the overall party experience more than the actual challenges do.

## Creating Sustainable Hosting Practices for Long-Term Success

The ultimate goal of developing hosting confidence is creating lasting practices that allow you to enjoy bringing people together over the long term rather than burning out from unsustainable hosting approaches. This requires honest assessment of your motivations, capacity, and goals for social entertaining.

Lasting hosting means finding rhythms and patterns that work with your life circumstances, energy levels, and relationship priorities rather than imposing external standards about hosting frequency or party size. Some people thrive hosting monthly gatherings, others prefer seasonal celebrations, and some find quarterly intimate dinners more manageable.

I've developed hosting schedules that align with my natural energy cycles and life patterns rather than social expectations about entertaining frequency. I host more during seasons when I have higher energy and fewer competing obligations, and I scale back during periods when other life priorities need attention.

The financial sustainability of hosting practices matters as much as energy sustainability. Developing hosting approaches that work within your budget without creating financial stress or requiring elaborate spending helps maintain long-term hosting enjoyment rather than associating entertaining with financial pressure.

Relationship sustainability means hosting in ways that strengthen rather than strain your friendships and family connections. This might mean being honest about your hosting capacity, asking for help when needed, and choosing gathering types that genuinely serve relationship building rather than social obligation fulfillment.

The most important insight about hosting confidence is that it's not about becoming someone different; it's about becoming more skilled at expressing your natural strengths through thoughtful entertaining. When your hosting style aligns with your personality and values, bringing people together becomes a source of energy and satisfaction rather than a drain on your resources.

# Building Lasting Connections Through Thoughtful Hosting

Here is the secret that takes most hosts years to discover: the party is not the point. The party is the mechanism. What you're actually building, if you're doing this right, is a web of relationships, a reputation as someone worth knowing, and a community that didn't exist before you started bringing people together. That's a significant return on investment for someone who just wanted to have a few people over for dinner.

The thank-you text that changed how I think about hosting arrived three days after what I considered a completely ordinary dinner party. My friend Elena wrote: "I've been thinking about Saturday night. It wasn't just the food or the conversation, it was how you made space for everyone to be themselves. Marcus opened up about his career change in a way I've never heard before, and David shared that story about his dad that made us all cry. You create environments where real connection happens."

## Creating Meaningful Experiences That Align with Your Values

The most memorable gatherings aren't usually the most expensive or elaborate ones; they're the ones where something genuine happens between people. As an introvert host, your natural tendency toward depth over breadth, quality over quantity, and authentic interaction over surface-level entertainment creates ideal conditions for meaningful connection.

I've learned that meaningful experiences emerge from alignment between your personal values and your hosting choices. If you value intellectual curiosity, create opportunities for people to share ideas and learn from each other. If you value creativity, provide space for artistic expression or creative discussion. If you value community service, organize gatherings that include charitable elements or social impact activities.

When your hosting reflects what you genuinely care about, you attract guests who share those values and create gatherings where people can connect around shared principles rather than just shared social obligation. This leads to relationships that continue developing long after the party ends.

For example, if environmental sustainability matters to you, hosting gatherings that demonstrate lasting practices (local food, minimal waste, seasonal menus) creates conversation opportunities around shared environmental values. Guests who appreciate these elements often become lasting connections because you've identified common ground that goes deeper than social politeness.

If intellectual growth energizes you, hosting book discussions, documentary screenings, or skill-sharing gatherings creates frameworks for people to engage with ideas together. These types of gatherings often lead to ongoing study groups, collaborative projects, or mentorship relationships because they reveal intellectual compatibility and shared learning interests.

Professional communities appreciate hosting that supports career development while maintaining genuine personal connection. Gatherings that blend networking with meaningful social interaction (skill sharing, industry discussion, or collaborative problem solving) often lead to lasting professional relationships and collaboration opportunities.

The foundation of all of this is authenticity; your hosting values need to reflect your genuine interests rather than values you think you should have. When you host around things you care about, your enthusiasm becomes contagious and attracts people who share your passions.

# Following Up After Parties in Ways That Feel Natural

I'm usually too drained the day after a party to do much of anything. But I've found that one or two specific messages sent within a few days land better than any amount of general socializing I could force myself through.

The key is being specific, not prolific.

Specific appreciation messages work much better than generic thank-you notes because they show you were present and engaged during conversations. Instead of "Thanks for coming," try "I loved hearing about your photography project, I'd love to see some of your work when you're ready to share it" or "That story about your grandmother's garden had me thinking about family traditions all week."

These messages serve multiple purposes: they show genuine interest in people's lives, they reference specific conversations that demonstrate your attention, and they often provide a natural opening for ongoing connection around shared interests or experiences.

Photo sharing creates ongoing connection opportunities when handled thoughtfully. Choose a few good photos that capture genuine moments or interesting conversations, then share them with people or small groups rather than mass distribution. This gives you reasons to continue conversations while providing people with visual memories of positive experiences.

Supporting connections extends party relationships beyond your immediate gathering. If you introduced people who seemed to connect well, following up to see how their conversation developed shows thoughtful hosting and often leads to gratitude from both parties. "Did you and Marcus ever connect about that hiking trail recommendation?" shows ongoing attention to relationship building.

Information sharing based on party conversations demonstrates that you listened and remembered what people cared about. If someone mentioned looking for book recommendations, restaurant suggestions, or professional contacts, following up with relevant information shows thoughtful attention and often leads to deeper ongoing connection.

The timing of follow-up matters more than the elaborateness. Simple messages sent within a few days feel natural and connected to the gathering experience. Follow-up that's delayed for weeks loses connection to the original interaction and feels obligatory rather than genuine.

I also use post-party follow-up to gather information that improves future hosting. Not formal feedback requests, but casual conversations about what people enjoyed, what worked well, and what they'd be interested in for future gatherings. This information helps refine your hosting approach while showing guests that their experience matters to you.

## Building a Reputation as a Thoughtful, Reliable Host

The reputation builds without you trying. People talk. I've had people I barely knew show up at gatherings saying a mutual friend told them they had to come. You don't manufacture that; you just keep doing the thing consistently and it accumulates. This reputation becomes valuable both personally and professionally because it positions you as someone who supports connection and creates positive experiences for others.

Consistency in hosting quality matters more than frequency or elaborateness. People remember hosts who reliably create comfortable, enjoyable experiences more than hosts who occasionally throw impressive parties but sometimes fail to deliver positive experiences. Your reputation builds through accumulation of consistently positive hosting experiences.

The specific elements that build hosting reputation include reliability (people can count on your gatherings being well-planned and enjoyable), inclusivity (people feel welcomed and comfortable regardless of their social style), and authenticity (people experience genuine connection rather than artificial entertainment).

I've learned that word-of-mouth recommendations from satisfied guests create the most valuable hosting reputation. When people tell their friends about positive experiences at your gatherings, they're endorsing not just your party-throwing skills but your ability to create meaningful social experiences. This type of recommendation often leads to relationship opportunities beyond just hosting.

Professional benefits of thoughtful hosting reputation include enhanced networking capabilities, leadership recognition, and relationship-building skills that transfer to workplace contexts. People who can create comfortable, productive social environments often find these skills valuable in professional settings as well.

The hosting reputation that matters most is the one you build within communities that genuinely matter to you. Being known as the person who throws great book club discussions, excellent post-hike gatherings, or memorable birthday celebrations within your specific interest communities creates more meaningful opportunities than generic party-throwing reputation.

Your hosting reputation requires ongoing attention to guest experience and continuous improvement in your skills. This doesn't mean constantly increasing complexity or expense, but rather refining your approach based on what works well and what could be improved.

The reputation development process includes learning from other respected hosts in your communities, seeking feedback about your hosting approach, and staying attentive to changing needs and preferences among your regular guests. Hosting skills that worked well five years ago might need updating as your friend groups evolve or your living situation changes.

## Inspiring Other Introverts to Embrace Entertaining

A few people have told me they started hosting after seeing how I did it. Not because my parties were fancy (they weren't), but because it looked like something they could actually do. That's been more satisfying than any compliment about the food.

I've found that many introverts avoid hosting because they assume it requires extroverted skills and energy levels they don't possess. When they experience thoughtful, comfortable hosting that aligns with introvert strengths, they often realize that successful entertaining is more about creating good environments than maintaining high personal energy.

Sharing hosting knowledge with other introverts creates supportive communities where people can develop entertaining skills together rather than feeling isolated in their hosting attempts. This might involve informal mentoring relationships, hosting skill sharing, or collaborative hosting arrangements where people support each other's social gatherings.

The demonstration of hosting practices that last helps other introverts understand that entertaining doesn't have to be draining or overwhelming. When they see you hosting regularly while maintaining energy and enthusiasm, they learn that durable approaches to entertaining are possible with appropriate planning and boundary management.

Teaching specific introvert hosting techniques (energy management, conversation facilitation, preparation systems) provides practical knowledge that helps other introverts develop confidence in their own hosting abilities. These skills transfer well because they're based on personality strengths rather than generic party planning advice.

Collaborative hosting opportunities let less experienced introverts learn hosting skills through partnership rather than solo trial and error. Co-hosting arrangements, potluck organization, or shared event planning all provide learning opportunities while distributing hosting workload among multiple people.

The modeling of authentic hosting styles shows other introverts that successful entertaining doesn't require personality transformation. When they see you being genuinely yourself while creating positive experiences for others, they gain permission to explore hosting approaches that align with their own natural strengths and interests.

Different introvert communities benefit from different types of hosting inspiration and support. Some people need practical skill development and systematic approaches to party planning. Others need emotional support and encouragement to attempt hosting despite social anxiety. Still others need examples of hosting styles that align with their specific interests and values.

The ripple effect of introvert hosting inspiration often extends beyond just encouraging more people to host parties. People who develop confidence in creating social experiences often become better at supporting collaboration in professional settings, organizing community activities, and building relationships in various life contexts.

## Creating Legacy Through Meaningful Connection

The ultimate goal of thoughtful hosting isn't throwing impressive parties or building social media presence; it's creating opportunities for genuine human connection that enriches people's lives in lasting ways. The relationships formed, ideas shared, and experiences created at your gatherings can have impacts that extend far beyond the immediate social experience.

I've learned to think about hosting as relationship building rather than entertainment provision. When you create environments where people can meet others who share their interests, values, or life situations, you're potentially supporting friendships, romantic relationships, professional partnerships, or creative collaborations that might never have developed otherwise.

I keep a running note on my phone, not systematically, just when something occurs to me, of relationships that started at my table. The couple who met at my birthday party for Marcus. The business partnership that started when I seated two people next to each other because they'd both mentioned starting companies that year. The friendship between two women who discovered over dinner that they'd grown up in the same small town in Ohio and never crossed paths. I didn't engineer any of those. I just created a room where they could happen.

I once got a wedding invitation from two people who met at my book club dinner. I'd put them next to each other because they'd both mentioned recently moving to the city and seeming a little lonely. I remembered nothing about the deliberate seating until their save-the-date arrived. Sometimes the hosting work is so quiet you forget you did it.

Documentation of meaningful hosting experiences helps you appreciate the cumulative impact of your entertaining efforts. Keeping track of relationships that developed, projects that emerged, or connections that strengthened as a result of your gatherings provides perspective on the long-term value of your hosting investment.

The legacy aspect of hosting also includes the hosting skills and approaches you share with others, particularly other introverts who benefit from your example and guidance. When you help someone else develop confidence in creating meaningful social experiences, you're multiplying the impact of your own hosting development.

Different types of meaningful connection emerge from different hosting approaches. Intimate dinner parties often build deep personal friendships and emotional support networks. Professional gatherings might lead to career advancement opportunities and collaborative projects. Creative community hosting often inspires artistic partnerships and creative growth.

Meaningful hosting legacy develops through consistency and authenticity rather than any single impressive event. Small, regular gatherings that consistently create positive experiences often have more cumulative impact than occasional elaborate parties that don't reflect genuine hosting values.

The gatherings I'm most proud of aren't the elaborate ones. They're the Tuesday night dinners for four people that became a standing thing. The annual birthday dinner that someone told me they plan their year around. The low-stakes repetition that turned acquaintances into friends. That's the actual output of consistent hosting. Not impressive parties. A community that didn't exist before you started.

# Planning Templates and Checklists

Everything in this book eventually boils down to this chapter. The timelines, the checklists, the budget frameworks: it's all here in usable form. Think of this as the part where you stop reading about hosting and start actually doing something about it.

The dinner party that finally convinced me to create systematic planning templates wasn't a disaster; it was a success that I almost ruined through my own disorganization. I was hosting eight people for my friend Sarah's birthday, and everything went perfectly: the food was delicious, conversations flowed naturally, and people stayed late because they were genuinely enjoying themselves. But I spent the entire evening stressed and distracted because I kept worrying that I'd forgotten something important.

I had no clear timeline for when things needed to happen, no system for tracking RSVPs, and no checklist to reassure me that I'd handled all the essential details. Instead of enjoying my own party, I was mentally cycling through endless possibilities of what might have slipped through the cracks. The irony was that everything was fine; I just had no systematic way to know that everything was fine.

## Detailed Timelines That Account for Prep and Recovery Time

The templates that actually helped me weren't party timelines; they were energy timelines. When do I need to be completely done with prep so I have 30 minutes to decompress before anyone arrives? When do I build in the kitchen break? When does cleanup stop for the night so I'm not wrecked tomorrow? That's the timeline worth building.

I've developed full-cycle timeline planning that covers three phases: Preparation (everything that happens before guests arrive), Hosting (the party itself and immediate cleanup), and

Recovery (the time needed to return to normal life after hosting). Each phase has different energy requirements and needs appropriate time allocation.

The Preparation phase timeline works backward from guest arrival time, with built-in buffers for things taking longer than expected. I always build in at least 30 minutes before guests arrive when all major preparation is complete and I can shift from preparation mode to hosting mode. This transition time is crucial for introverts because it allows mental adjustment from task-focused energy to social-focused energy.

Here's my standard dinner party timeline template for eight people: Two weeks before, send invitations, plan menu, create shopping lists. One week before, grocery shop for non-perishables, confirm final guest count, prepare any make-ahead dishes. Three days before, final grocery shopping, major prep cooking, space setup that doesn't interfere with daily life. Day before, final food preparation, complete space setup, personal preparation. Day of, finishing touches only, personal care, mental transition to hosting mode.

Good timeline planning feels like having more time rather than less time because tasks are distributed appropriately rather than compressed into frantic last-minute preparation. When each task has adequate time allocation, nothing feels rushed or overwhelming.

Different types of gatherings require different timeline structures based on their complexity and your experience level. Casual gatherings with simple food can have shorter preparation timelines but still benefit from systematic planning. Formal dinner parties need longer preparation periods but most tasks can be completed well in advance.

Holiday parties require extended timelines because they often involve special foods, decorations, or traditions that need extra preparation time. They also compete with other seasonal obligations, so timeline planning needs to account for limited availability during busy holiday periods.

Professional events might need longer planning timelines for coordination with attendees' schedules, venue booking, or special equipment needs. Gaming events might require time for game selection, rule review, and equipment setup that's specific to planned activities.

The Recovery phase timeline is often overlooked but equally important for lasting hosting. This includes immediate post-party cleanup, next-day tasks like returning borrowed items or storing leftovers, and personal recovery time before resuming normal social obligations. I always block the day after hosting for low-key activities and minimal social commitments.

I maintain separate timeline templates for different party types and guest counts, refined through experience with what works for my space, cooking abilities, and energy patterns. These templates eliminate the mental work of recreating planning schedules for each gathering while providing proven frameworks that reduce preparation stress.

## PARTY DAY CHECKLIST (print and post in your kitchen)

### SPACE

☐ Tables and chairs arranged

☐ Bathroom clean and stocked (extra toilet paper, hand soap, towel)

☐ Candles or lighting set up

☐ Music playlist tested and queued

☐ Coat area designated and clear

☐ Any fragile/personal items put away

### FOOD AND DRINK

☐ All prep complete, nothing left that requires active decisions

☐ Serving dishes set out and labeled if needed

□ Wine/beverages chilled or accessible

□ Ice in freezer or bought

□ Bottle opener on the counter

□ Non-alcoholic options visible

**HOST PREP**

□ Outfit ready

□ Phone charged

□ One recharge spot identified (kitchen, back step, bathroom)

□ Co-host briefed if applicable

□ Energy check: do I have 30 minutes of quiet before guests arrive?

**THE RULE:** If it's not done one hour before guests arrive, it doesn't get done. Unfinished prep is less noticeable than a stressed host.

**BUDGET TEMPLATE: DINNER FOR 8**

**CASUAL DINNER (target: $80-100 total)**

Food: $40-50

Protein/main: $20-25

Vegetables/sides: $10-12

Bread/extras: $5-8

Dessert: $8-10

Drinks: $25-30

Wine (2-3 bottles): $18-24

Beer or alternative: $6-10

Non-alcoholic: already in house, or $3-5

Supplies: $8-12

Ice: $3

Candles/flowers: $5-8

Napkins if needed: $3

Contingency (10%): $8-10

## SPECIAL OCCASION DINNER (target: $120-150 total)

Food: $60-70

Drinks: $40-50 (better wine, maybe cocktail ingredients)

Flowers/décor: $15-20

Supplies: $10-15

Contingency: $12-15

## COST PER PERSON BENCHMARKS

Casual dinner: $10-13/person

Special occasion: $15-20/person

If you're over $20/person for a home dinner, check the drink budget first; that's usually where the math goes sideways.

### Budget Worksheets with Contingency Planning

Budget planning for parties involves much more complexity than just adding up food and drink costs. Effective budget worksheets need to account for all actual expenses, provide frameworks for cost control decisions, and include contingency funds for unexpected expenses that always seem to arise.

I use a category-based budgeting system that breaks party costs into manageable segments: Food (including appetizers, main courses, sides, desserts), Beverages (alcoholic and non-alcoholic), Supplies (disposable items, decorations, serving pieces), and Contingency (15% of total budget for unexpected expenses or upgrades).

The Food category requires the most detailed planning because costs can vary dramatically based on menu choices, guest count, and quality levels. I break food costs into subcategories: Proteins (usually the most expensive component), Produce (vegetables, fruits, herbs), Pantry items (grains, dairy, condiments), and Special ingredients (items I don't normally stock).

For different dietary needs within your guest list, budget planning becomes more complex but also more important. Alternative protein options for vegetarians, gluten-free ingredients for celiac guests, or specialty items for other dietary restrictions all need budget allocation to prevent last-minute expensive shopping.

Beverage budgeting depends heavily on your guest demographics and party type. Wine-focused groups have different consumption patterns than beer-focused groups. Professional gatherings might require higher-quality alcohol options than casual friend gatherings. Gaming events might emphasize non-alcoholic beverages that don't interfere with concentration.

The Supplies category includes both obvious items (napkins, plates if using disposables) and easily forgotten items (ice, coffee filters, trash bags, cleaning supplies for spills). I maintain a master supplies list that I customize for each party type rather than trying to remember all necessary items for each gathering.

Contingency planning involves both financial buffers and decision frameworks for when costs exceed planned amounts. I identify "budget flexibility points" where I can scale up or down depending on how costs develop. Maybe I plan simple cookies but research bakery options if I'm under budget. Or I choose a menu that works for 6-10 people depending on final guest count.

Seasonal cost variations affect budget planning significantly. Summer parties might cost less due to abundant fresh produce but more if air conditioning costs increase. Winter parties might have higher food costs but lower beverage costs if people prefer warm drinks. Holiday parties compete with seasonal price increases for many party staples.

I track actual costs against planned budgets to improve future budget accuracy. This data helps me understand which categories consistently cost more than expected, which menu choices provide good value, and how different party types compare financially.

# Go Throw a Party

You made it to the end of the book, which means one of two things: you read straight through, in which case you are a very committed introvert, or you skipped around and landed here looking for a satisfying conclusion. Either way, what follows is less a summary and more a send-off.

Six months after that first disastrous dinner party where I hid in my kitchen stress-eating appetizers, I threw what I still consider one of my best gatherings ever. It was a simple autumn dinner for eight people, the same number that had overwhelmed me before, but everything felt completely different.

I wasn't frantically managing every conversation or apologizing for imaginary hosting failures. I wasn't exhausted from performing an extroverted version of myself or worried that people weren't having fun. Instead, I was present at my own party, enjoying genuine conversations with people I cared about in a space I'd thoughtfully prepared.

The difference wasn't that I'd suddenly become more social or developed magical party-planning abilities. The difference was that I'd learned to host as myself, using my natural introvert strengths instead of fighting against them, creating systems that supported my energy instead of depleting it, and focusing on authentic connection instead of impressive entertainment.

That evening, watching my friends laugh over stories I'd never heard before, seeing new friendships develop between people I'd introduced, and feeling genuinely energized by the social connection I'd supported, I finally understood what hosting could be when it aligned with who I was.

Here's what I know from years of doing this: the first party is the hardest. Not because it goes badly (it usually doesn't), but because you don't have evidence yet that you can do it. After the first one, you have evidence. After the third one, you have a system. After the tenth one, you have something you actually look forward to.

The people in your life who have never once been to your home for dinner: they're waiting for an invitation. They won't say so. But they are.

You now have the frameworks, the scripts, the checklists, and the permission. The rest is just picking a date, inviting a few people, and making something to eat.

Go throw a party.

# Books by Richard Lowe

See books by Richard Lowe at
https://masterofworlds.com


Get free publishing insights and industry updates at
https://thewritingking.substack.com


For ghostwriting and book coaching services see
https://thewritingking.com